Paul Bunyan Lives!

And Other Tales from the Natural World

Michael O'Rourke

Plain View Press
P.O. 42255
Austin, TX 78704

plainviewpress.net
sb@plainviewpress.net
512-441-2452

ISBN: 978-1-935514-43-5
Library of Congress Number: 2010929235

Cover art: Janell O'Rourke.
Cover design by Susan Bright.

Acknowledgments

"Little Creek" was first published in *The North American Review*; "Wrecklamation" in *Isotope*; "Fish Story" in *ISLE: Interdisciplinary Studies in Literature and Environment*; "Out of the Air" (as "Just Outside") in *ISLE*; "Pocket Wildernesses, and the Good Dr Pepper Defiled" in *The North American Review*; "Paul Bunyan Lives!" in *CNS: Capitalism Nature Socialism*; "Desert Ships" in *Snowy Egret*; "Laughing Gulls and Chameleons" in *High Plains Literary Review*; "Old News" in *ISLE*; and "This Rock" in *Cimarron Review*.

for Michelle

Though much was lost, much remained –
though much was lost.

Edward Abbey
The Monkey Wrench Gang

Contents

ONE:
LAND O LAKES

Little Creek

*T*he little creek that winds past my apartment building ends, in a sense, where it begins – in the underground drainage system of the university where I teach. Its origins are in the network of streams and caves that coil through the subsurface limestone in this region, which was formed in ancient seas about 350,000,000 years ago. That subsurface now is overlain with the blacktop of the basketball arena parking lot, formed about 30 years ago, and with the network of campus and city streets that stretch beyond. The creek's beginnings are now pipes, its point of emergence a concrete culvert, its flow-rate determined by urban runoff. It makes a continuous getaway from this source – wriggles free – and yet remains, in a sense, a fugitive on the run.

Its name is, in fact, Little Creek.

Well, not exactly; creeks are cagey.

The three-quarter-mile snippet that loops around my street, creating a cul-de-sac, doesn't even appear on topographical maps. It tiptoes past apartments, small businesses, a few houses; slips through brush and thickets; then ducks behind a rock and dives underground. It *seems* to reappear on the other side of a rise about a half-mile farther north (where the mapped Little Creek begins) in the form of a streambed that winds through woods and pastureland for another mile until water surfaces again from beneath the half-exposed roots of a listing cottonwood. In reality, however, it hangs a sharp east, burrows for a couple of miles beneath the fluster and fuss of the small American city overhead, and re-emerges on the side of a hill at the base of an outcropping of rock, where it escapes, as if by design, the housing development above into the quiet of an undisturbed glen. Here its name is not "little" anything but Big Spring (at least to the locals, for again it isn't mapped), having roughly doubled in volume and pouring from the side of that hill. It then either immediately intersects with the officially acknowledged stream it will become, or soon but not immediately, or it *is* that acknowledged stream, depending upon the maps you read, the ground you tread, and you – whereupon, a meandering ten miles later, and now returning west, "it," the official stream (which actually is a fork of a larger fork of a larger river, but that's another...river), joins its companion branch, one of whose tributaries, also hailing from the east, and "starting" at that cottonwood, is Little Creek.

Yes, cagey.

○

My three-quarter-mile snippet doesn't actually have a name, not even to the locals, but I've dubbed it Little Creek because it seems to flow to that stream and because, according to a geologist friend, it likely once did. Streams, both above ground and below, merge and divide; land rises and falls; and there is evidence, says my friend, of an ancient valley connecting "my" Little Creek with the one on the map. To the extent that streams can be dated at all – since they do shift around so much – this prehistoric creek existed one to six million years ago, quenching the thirsts of woolly mammoths and saber-toothed tigers. Time passed, water flowed, and then at some indistinct subsequent point, having reached soluble limestone, the creek tunneled its way underground, burrowing off in a different direction and leaving my snippet behind like the tip of a tail.

Its environment, of course, has changed markedly during the period of time following that small event. The only mammoths in the area now are the bulldozers lumbering over the ground outside my backdoor, making way for more apartments, and the saber-toothed tigers have since shrunk, although they still like to drink, as do my two, at the creek's banks. The trees lining those banks – locust, elm, box elder, sycamore, sassafras, yellow poplar – are all native to this part of the country, but they suggest the hardwood forest of which their forebears were once a part the way a thread suggests the blanket that once comprised it. The creek itself does contain at least one snapping turtle, who I saw peering up at me from its greeny depths one day, but seems richer now in trash forms than life forms. You could furnish a humble dwelling or construct a vehicle of sorts from the domestic debris scattered along its course. It's a depository now, a drainage ditch and garbage dump, superfluous to its environment except as a siphon. Once upon a time it was an important part of its surroundings; now it's surrounded and ignored.

A Fun Karts franchise ("Go-Carts and Batting Cages, Bumper-Boats and Video Games, Big-Screen TV") is one of its neighbors. It sits on the creek's west bank where the creek emerges from the culvert that channels it under the street next to the parking lot that overlays its subsurface beginnings. Yellow batting-cage balls that have escaped from their cages tumble down the creekbank and are carried, when it rains, downstream. They come to rest wherever they've landed when the water level drops – half-submerged in stagnant backwaters, half-hidden in viney thickets, wedged between two rocks or two chunks of concrete. If I were an enterprising ten-year-old, I'd collect those balls and sell them back to the Fun Karts man: adventure and commerce combined. But adventure for the kids at Fun Karts isn't exploring a winding creek; it's buzzing around in circles on a blacktop track. It's floating in plastic boats in an above-ground metal tank and peering, not at turtles, but dancing electrons. It's hitting plastic balls with aluminum bats in wire cages, and never wondering where the balls that escape end up.

Then there are the "Eagle Creek" apartments on the stream's opposite bank (mine are a "Village" farther downstream) that, no, aren't named for the creek since the creek is nameless except in the would-be poetical mind of some developer, nor for the eagles in the area, the sightings of which exist somewhere on the outside limits of rare, but for the college's sports mascot, the golden eagle, a purported specimen of which sits stuffed in the student union – purported since it's actually, a birder friend tells me, an immature bald. My two-story brick "village" sits on a bend of not-Eagle Creek, not-feeling very communal, the tenants coming and going without speaking, a short nod the most that is usually ever exchanged. This is possibly the result of the climate of fear and anxiety created by the message loudly painted on the apartment dumpster: TeNATs ONLY WILL BE PROSCUTeD. I've not witnessed any arrests, but our ovate landlady is careful to maintain an air of officialdom about the place by not *walking* the thirty or forty yards from her townhouse across the parking lot to her office, but *driving* it in her gleaming, crimson Jeep Cherokee.

Has she ever wanted to look at the creek?

○

But creeks are cagey.

Soon after it gives the town the slip by tunneling underground, then re-emerging as Big Spring, it hooks up with (or becomes) the East Blackburn Fork of the Roaring River. Its confidence restored, it trips along through pastures and fields till it reaches the Blackburn Fork, where it becomes officially "scenic" – and actually too, complete with swift-running water and even trout. Next it meets the Roaring River, which isn't roaring at this point in its journey but more resting-up-from-all-the-exertion, rounds a couple of bends and opens suddenly on the Cumberland River, a considerably larger affair on its way – by an exceedingly serpentine route – to the fabled Ohio. Back and forth it goes, dipping south, then angling north, taking its time for hundreds of miles on its anything-but-how-the-crow-flies westward course, until at tiny Smithland, Kentucky, with no more fanfare than is provided by a pair of fishermen afloat in their skiff, it joins the Ohio.

But now the pace picks up. No sooner does it reach the Ohio (giving Paducah a passing glance) than the mighty Mississippi comes into view, a horizon of water thundering single-mindedly south. It joins the torrent just below Cairo and is swept along past Hickman, Caruthersville, Osceola – towns and cities being left behind like backwater driftwood. Memphis soon appears and is just as quickly gone; Vicksburg is a distant memory of a distant battle. And all the while the momentum builds as other rivers join the march – the Arkansas, the Yazoo, the Red. What's the hurry? Why this headlong rush through stalwart locks and dams, past bridges, levees, docks, pleasant riverfront parks? Where are we headed with such inexorable resolve? Then New Orleans, then the delta, and yes, now we know.

There it is: the Gulf of Mexico, the sea.

Wrecklamation

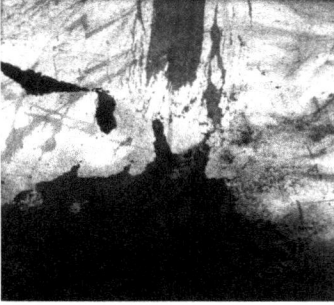

"*M*ight be interesting to revisit that," said my friend Tom.

I'd been telling him about my memory of having written, at the age of sixteen or seventeen (fifteen? eighteen? anyway, thirty-some years ago), a letter to the editor of the *Saturday Evening Post* about some sort of environmental issue – I couldn't remember what – which they'd published.

It was my "first publication," I remember my parents and me saying, and I remember seeing it and being pleased – but I didn't save it, apparently because the Great Novels with which I would shortly be gracing the world would reduce this first minor achievement to the tiniest of footnotes.

The letter (I'm telling Tom) was short because I knew, having read them, that some letters were cut, and I didn't want mine cut. I also didn't want to be labeled a kid, as routinely happened when they published a kid's letter ("Sarah Jones, 12 years old"): this would be a letter from an *adult*. Whatever article I had read had made me angry, and so I'd reached for the sarcasm – something about tearing down the Rockies, something about melting glaciers?

"But that's all I can remember. And I don't recall the article itself."

"Might be interesting to revisit that."

O

The cover story for the August 12, 1967 issue of the *Saturday Evening Post* was "The Hidden Evils of LSD" by Bill Davidson. I probably read it (I was seventeen and knew a couple of kids who had dropped acid), but don't remember it – though it may have been partly responsible for my trying nothing stronger, a couple of years later, than mescaline.

I probably also read an Oriana Fallaci piece entitled "My Name is Twiggy" because it was short and Twiggy was my age (and astoundingly ignorant: "Twiggy, do you know what happened at Hiroshima?" "Where's that?" "In Japan." "No, I've never heard of it. What happened there?"); may have read the editorial on Vietnam ("One of the great illusions about our struggle in Vietnam has always been that it could be won fairly easily"); probably didn't read (but Eugene McCarthy would soon wake me up politically) Stewart Alsop's "Affairs of State" piece on Rockefeller's presidential chances in '68 ("Richard Nixon's candidacy is visibly fading...The notion of [Ronald Reagan], totally inexperienced in foreign affairs, as the standard-bearer of the Grand Old Party would surely appall a lot of Republicans") – but the article I now know I did read was "'Don't flood our Grand Canyon'" by John Bird.

Remember? Or not. Know about it? Or not. I didn't really remember it clearly myself – even after I found my letter and then, three issues earlier, the article – but I'd read about it in Marc Reisner's superb book *Cadillac Desert* and "remembered" it in that sense.

"The battle over the Grand Canyon dams was the conservation movement's coming of age," says Reisner on page 285. Thirty-some years later I discovered – quite to my surprise – that my "first publication" had fired a small shot in that battle.

O

It was a battle a long time coming.

The U.S. Bureau of Reclamation (or, as Edward Abbey liked to spell it, "Wrecklamation") was formed in 1902 following Congress's passage of the Reclamation Act. The idea was to "reclaim" the arid West with various federal water projects to make it habitable for humans – as if mean old Mother Nature had somehow taken it from us and made it dry, and now we had to take it back and make it wet. John Wesley Powell – who knew a tad more about the West than your average senator, having explored the Colorado River in 1869 from Green River, Wyoming, to the end of the Grand Canyon – had suggested that Western settlement proceed carefully and thoughtfully – for example, state formation around watersheds – but Congress would have none of that: growing fruit trees in the desert and erecting cities where no city should be was more...Manifest Destiny-ish.

The first big recipient of Reclamation largess was California. At a time when its sister states in the Colorado River Basin (Nevada, Arizona, New Mexico, Utah, Colorado, and Wyoming) were still in their infancy, California was growing like an adolescent on steroids and needing more water for its desert agriculture and its city-that-shouldn't-be-there, Los

Angeles. Having already stolen, albeit "legally," the Owens River to the north from the farmers in that valley (by buying up their water rights for what they were told was a local irrigation project), L.A. next looked to the east to the only river of any consequence left to tap, the Colorado. A monster dam with a monster reservoir was what it and the Imperial Valley had in mind, but there was a problem: the other states weren't pleased about the prospect of Big Sis drinking more than her share.

The Colorado River Compact of 1922, which divided the river's water among the seven interested states by dividing the states into Upper and Lower Colorado River Basins,[1] with each basin receiving roughly half, was supposed to solve this problem, and others, but it solved very little. For one thing, it split the water between the arbitrarily designated basins, not the states, leaving the states to fight it out over their individual allotments, which they then proceeded to do. For another, the annual allotment to each basin of 7.5 million acre-feet was way too high, having been based on Reclamation's claim that the annual average flow of the river was 17.5 million acre-feet, which was based on studies conducted during a series of unusually wet years. Ergo, the states were being promised water the Colorado didn't have, which resulted in its being labeled a "deficit" river (just doesn't know how to budget itself, that river), and ultimately resulted in the pathetic fact that the mighty Colorado, which for no small amount of geologic time emptied into the Gulf of California, now gasps its last breath before it gets there.

(Brief digression. Something else happened in 1922. Aldo Leopold and his brother traveled to the Colorado River Delta and explored it by canoe, which Leopold later wrote about in his essay "The Green Lagoons." They found waterfowl of every description, bobcats, burro deer, even the felt presence of jaguar:

> The still waters were of a deep emerald hue, colored by algae, I suppose, but no less green for all that. A verdant wall of mesquite and willow separated the channel from the thorny desert beyond. At each bend we saw egrets standing in the pools ahead, each white statue matched by its white reflection. Fleets of cormorants drove their black prows in quest of skittering mullets; avocets, willets, and yellowlegs dozed one-legged on the bars; mallards, widgeons, and teal sprang skyward in alarm. As the birds took to the air, they accumulated in a small cloud ahead, there to settle, or to break back to our rear. When a troop of egrets settled on a far green willow, they looked like a premature snowstorm. (151)

A bit of "history," I guess you could say.)

Also, the Indian tribes (surprised?) weren't even mentioned in the Compact. And Mexico's allotment of 1.5 million acre-feet would be so saline by the time it got there that it would kill the crops it was meant to sustain.

But after six years of squabbling, six of the seven states signed the Compact (Arizona, still suspicious of California, refused), and Hoover Dam was built (in five lightning-fast years, from 1931 to '36), and California was also given the All-American Canal, which siphons water from the Colorado just above the Mexican border to the Imperial Valley.

Then the Bureau of Reclamation handed California the monumentally ambitious – and monumentally expensive – Central Valley Project (which transformed the great Central Valley of California, home to millions upon millions of wintering waterfowl, into vast corporate "farms"), and "compact" isn't quite the word that describes the mood of the other states at this point, especially those in the upper basin.

Three massive projects for California, zip for the upper basin. Of course, the upper basin states were higher, colder, their soils less fertile, and their growing seasons shorter; because of that, only lower-value crops like alfalfa and wheat were feasible; because of *that*, the irrigation projects the states wanted the Bureau to build could not possibly pay for themselves (i.e. the crops would cost far more to grow than they were worth); often *these same crops* were being grown in surplus in the East, or, to add insanity to absurdity, farmers in the East were being paid *not* to grow them; but the upper basin states had been promised their 7.5 million acre-feet and, by God, they were going to get it!

(Which suggests another problem with the Compact: half and half was dumb. If irrigated agriculture makes sense at all, and most of the time it doesn't, the warmer, more fertile lower basin should have been allotted more water than the upper...but that would be thinking rationally, not politically.)

So how do you pay for irrigation projects that can't pay for themselves, hence should never have been built because they can't pay for themselves? Answer: cash register dams.

Dams – low dams – were originally built just for irrigation. Then in the 1920s it was discovered that high dams could also generate electricity via the release of the stored water through turbines.

Well, how about building dams mostly for electricity?

Cash register dams (the Bureau's own term) was Reclamation's backasswards solution to the building of pork barrel water projects that made no sense: throw up a dam in some canyon somewhere, and pay for Senator X's pet porker through the sale of the electricity the dam generates. Since building magnificent dams was what Reclamation engineers lived for, "river-basin accounting," as they called it, was not only a solution, it was the perfect justification: now the Bureau *had* to build dams, lots of dams, to pay for pointless water projects that were sure to bankrupt the farmers who benefitted from them if the farmers weren't bailed out by the federal government.

To make it sound important, the scheme had to have a name, of course, so that everyone but a few grumbling conservationists would be fooled.

"Cash Register Dam Project"? "Pork Barrel Bail-Out Project?"? "Screw the American Taxpayer Project"?

No: the "Colorado River Storage Project," and quit making fun.

○

The infamous Glen Canyon Dam (completed in 1963), which drowned the incomparable Glen Canyon, so named by John Wesley Powell for its quiet, infinitely varied beauty, was one of ten planned Colorado River Storage Project dams. All ten wouldn't be built, but in the meantime Arizona was growing increasingly annoyed over something else that hadn't been built (but would be) – the Central Arizona Project (CAP).

California was happy, the upper basin was semi-happy (projects proceeding slowly), but Arizona, it felt, had been getting the shaft. For decades CAP had been in the talking-and-arguing stages but had yet to be authorized.

What was it?...is it? Just a simple little plan (eventually costing $4.7 billion) to pump water from you-know-what river *uphill* 1200 feet and then down into central Arizona so that Arizona's desert-farmers – who were siphoning water for their crops from finite underground aquifers, a customary practice in the Southwest – could emulate their subsidized millionaire colleagues in California's Central Valley. Phoenix and Tucson would get some water, too, but CAP was mainly conceived as an irrigation project.

And how would this monstrosity be financed?

A couple of cash register dams, of course.

And where would these dams be built?

Well, for such a grand undertaking, grand vision is required. What say we put them in the Grand Canyon?

O

Glen Canyon Dam had been a compromise. Echo Park in northwest Colorado, where the Yampa River joins the Green, had been slated for a dam, but Echo Park was also in Dinosaur National Monument and a favorite haunt of David Brower, who was executive director of the then relatively small Sierra Club. Brower went before Congress and, virtually single-handedly, using the Bureau of Reclamation's own inaccurate numbers against it, fought the dam off.

But this was the late 1950s – pre-Clean Air and Water Acts, pre-Endangered Species Act, pre-environmental impact statement requirements – and you didn't get something like a stupid dam canceled without a trade-off. The trade-off was Glen Canyon, which was not a part of the National Park System, which was very remote, and which Brower had not yet seen. When he did see it, on a river trip before the dam's gates were closed, he realized what he had traded...and the Grand Canyons dams had themselves an opponent.

The two dams – one in Marble Canyon, just east of Grand Canyon National Park, and one in Bridge Canyon [2], just west – would have bookended the park on both sides. No, they wouldn't have "flooded" the Grand Canyon (that was beyond even Reclamation's maniacal dreams). Yes, they would have flooded the lower reaches of it 90-plus miles in one direction and 40-plus miles in the other, and they would have negatively and permanently altered both the Grand Canyon and Colorado River ecosystems even more than the Glen Canyon plug already had.

The Sierra Club (which is now regarded by more "radical" environmental groups as not aggressive enough, but then, under Brower, *was* the aggressor) placed full-page ads in the *New York Times, Washington Post, Los Angeles Times,* and *San Francisco Chronicle* which asked, "Should we also flood the Sistine Chapel so tourists can get nearer the ceiling?" – a reference to one of Reclamation's arguments that powerboat owners would be able to do their beer-cooler, water-ski thing when the dams were built.

Emotional appeal? Of course. Acceptable tactic when you're dealing with the dam-crazed Bureau of Reclamation, its pork-barrel lackeys in the U.S. Congress, and a mostly uninformed American public?

Let's put it this way: David Brower, who died in 2000 at the age of 88, was a great man.

○

So Congress was deluged with letters, Congress does have a politician or two among its ranks, and this essay is about something that never happened.

Well, not quite...

The nearly $5 billion Central Arizona Project that the Grand Canyon dams were intended to finance [3] was finally completed in 1993. In his 1986 book, Reisner's sources predicted boondoggle: CAP water much more expensive for farmers, especially when the costs of the distribution systems were figured in, than simply continuing to mine the still large (albeit ever-diminishing) stores of groundwater.

That has largely happened. "Under-utilization" is a term often associated with CAP, and the result is the same old same-old: the American taxpayer ends up paying for outlandishly expensive Western water projects that never had a prayer of paying for themselves, while the recipients of the projects sit back and smile [4].

Whence *does* come the energy-for-sale that keeps the 14 pumping plants for CAP's 336-mile-long aqueduct pumping away?

Well, I guess you could say the red man lent a hand.

Black Mesa is a massive 3200-square-mile plateau that comprises nearly all of the Navajo and Hopi Indian Reservations in northeastern Arizona. Black Mesa itself is comprised of lots and lots of coal, about 21 billion tons of it, more coal in one spot than anywhere else in the country.

At about the time the dams were being defeated, both tribes were being talked into signing leases with the Peabody Coal Company of Kentucky (you know, where there's also lots of coal? and one of the most impoverished regions in America, called Appalachia?) for some of that Black Mesa black gold. How were they persuaded? The usual: jobs, economic prosperity, a rosy future – the American Dream with head feathers.

They signed (with assurances from the federal government, their legal trustee, that all was well), and Black Mesa became the site of the largest strip-mining operation in the U.S., supplying coal via electric railway to the Navajo Generating Station in northern Arizona near Page, and via slurry pipeline to the Mojave Generating Station in southern Nevada near Laughlin.

The Navajo Station became the substitute for the Grand Canyon dams – and the supplier of pollution for the Grand Canyon air – while the Mojave Station, besides assisting in that clear air menace, has another distinction: the above-mentioned slurry pipeline, the water for which is supplied by the Navajo Aquifer, which is the only water source for both tribes.

Peabody pumps (i.e. mines) from the aquifer over 1 billion gallons of perfectly potable water per year (that's 3 million gallons a day) for its wash-the-coal-down-a-pipe operation instead of transporting the coal by rail or truck. (The whole slurry-line thing was an experiment, you see, later to be magnanimously exported to "developing" countries.) The federal government had promised the tribes that should the mining endanger their groundwater supply, Peabody's water-wasting permit would be revoked. But though, according to the Natural Resources Defense Council...

> Water levels have decreased by more than 100 feet in some wells and discharge has slackened by more than 50 percent in the majority of monitored springs. There are reports that washes along the mesa's southern cliffs are losing outflow. And there are signs that the aquifer is being contaminated in places by low-quality water from overlying basins, which leak down in response to the stress caused by pumping. ("Drawdown" 2)

...though all of that has happened, though the tribes continue to petition the government to fulfill to them its obligation to protect their water supply, though Peabody refuses to ship the coal by any other means, the federal government – the Indians' legal trustee – has done nothing.

And all that American Dream stuff the Indians were painted pretty pictures of when they were duped into signing the lease?

Take a drive around northeastern Arizona sometime, and see how much milk and honey you can find.

○

In another excellent book, *A River No More*, author Philip Fradkin quotes Jeffrey Ingram, Southwest representative in 1967 of the Sierra Club, on dams in the Grand Canyon versus strip-mines and coal-fired power plants:

Suppose the dams are dropped from this legislation in favor of coal plants. Then we get air pollution. But if we give up coal plants for dams to save the air, we lose water through evaporation (which is one of the dams' hidden fuel costs – sedimentation is another). Yet if we save water by building coal plants instead of a dam, we use up coal. But if we then argue that we must save coal, a non-replenishable resource, and therefore build dams, we lose the river and canyon bottom, which puts us back where we were. (233)

Well articulated dilemma but false dilemma, since CAP, like so many Western water projects, should not have been built in the first place. Why were they built? Well, besides "I'll vote for your dam if you'll vote for mine" Congressional politics, besides money, besides greed, besides the stick-it-to-nature attitude of the human race in general, they were built, as we've seen, for irrigation. Irrigated agriculture accounts for 85-90% of all the water consumed in the West. The water "shortage" in the West is a shortage only because irrigated crops (mostly for cows) are grown where crops (and cows) don't belong. Without irrigated agriculture – which in the West means frequently surplus, and always subsidized, crops – everyone in the West could take hour-long showers, dig Olympic-sized swimming pools, and water their lawns till they shone emerald-green (and probably would, which would then result in a shortage, so I'm sorry I brought it up).

Irrigation destroys the land. Always. Sometimes quickly, sometimes slowly, but always.

Since arid lands that "need" irrigation are, yes, usually hot, evaporation, both from reservoirs and the irrigated lands themselves, results in water disappearing and the salts in the water staying behind. Also, soils that drain slowly, as do many of those in the West, get stuck with their dissolved salts when the water passes through. And finally and most critically, water taken from a river for irrigation that doesn't percolate into the (gradually more saline) aquifer below does eventually return to the (gradually more saline) river. As the irrigation process is repeated over and over again downstream (irrigate, leach out the salts, return...irrigate, leach out the salts, return...), the river's water becomes so saline that it is less than worthless: it kills.

Ever heard of the Fertile Crescent? You know, the Garden of Eden? Well, it isn't so fertile anymore, it's called Iraq, and the only thing it grows now, courtesy of a U.S. president named George W. Bush, is terrorists. Except for ancient Egypt, whose irrigation system worked in harmony with the Nile's annual silt-bearing spring floods, every ancient civilization dependent upon irrigation for its survival, from Mesopotamia to the Hohokam of the

American Southwest, eventually collapsed *because*, it is now believed, of the build-up of salts in those people's soils. Today, large areas of the formerly cultivated desert Southwest are dying proof of this theory. And they don't just return to being the deserts they were before – they're "history."

And dams?

Well, it seems we built a few too many – around 76,000 according to the U.S. Army Corps of Engineers' [5] "National Inventory of Dams" – and now the proverbial chickens are clucking their way home. Of course, most of those dams are relatively small – "only" about 2,000 fit into the Big Boy category (Reisner 104) – but it seems dams do more damage, and Big Boy dams a lot more damage, than anyone bothered to think about at the time (plus they're getting old), and now the word "decommission" is actually being uttered aloud in reference to some of them.

In the old days 1½ to 2 million salmon returned to the Snake River (largest tributary of the Columbia) every year to spawn. Now, because of four monster dams on the lower Snake [6], whose primary purpose is to provide the "seaport" of Lewiston, Idaho – 600 miles inland – with barges for the shipping of grain, the numbers are in the thousands, and salmon and steelhead trout are on the brink of extinction throughout the Columbia River Basin (americanrivers.org). Of course, shipping the grain by barge makes lots more sense. In 1999, for example, it cost $1.26 per ton to ship grain by rail, but with taxpayer subsidies figured in, only $13.89 per ton to ship it by barge. Meanwhile, the Columbia River fishing industry loses $500 million a year (that's around 25,000 jobs-worth), and the government's fishing treaties with the regional Indian tribes...well, as we all know, treaties were made to be broken. (Spain 3-5)

Back down in the Southwest, there's Glen Canyon Dam, which, together with its companion reservoir, and besides having drowned Glen Canyon...

✓. . . loses, through evaporation and bank seepage, almost one million acre-feet of water each year, which in dollar terms is more money lost than the dam makes in power sales (haven't we heard this before?)

✓ . . .is silting up – courtesy of one of the siltiest rivers in the world – at a rate equivalent to 30,000 dumptruck-loads of mud every day (100 million tons every year)

✓. . . and robs the river below the dam of 95% of its natural sediment, which has reduced the river's temperature from a former high of 85 degrees to a constant 46 degrees year-round and landed (ripple-ripple-ripple) at least 60 species of plants and animals on the Endangered and Threatened Species List.

But slowly, slowly things may be changing. Two hundred and twelve obsolete dams were removed between 1999 and 2005; 58 more were either removed or slated for removal in 2006 (americanrivers.org); in 1999 the biggest dam to date to be decommissioned, the Edwards Dam on the Kennebec River in Maine, was removed, restoring salmon and Atlantic sturgeon runs to that river for the first time in more than 150 years, and making everyone happy; California's bigger Matilija Dam, whose Ventura River reservoir is almost completely silted up, may not be far behind; there's a serious move afoot to decommission the defunct-except-for-the-salmon-they-kill Elwha and Glines dams in Washington State (they also happen to be in Olympic National Park); and even those four worst salmon-killing dams on the lower Snake, and even one of the biggest dams ever, the last big one to be built, and perhaps the most despised, Glen Canyon Dam on the Colorado, may someday, someday be put out of business...

Dream on, you pie-in-the-sky environmentalists.

Which reminds me – my letter.

Dear Sir:

For future water projects, why not melt all of those ridiculous glaciers in Glacier National Park, or blast apart those bothersome Rocky Mountains to get at the natural springs within them? All that original stuff is getting pretty old and worn out anyway.

Mike O'Rourke.

Wichita, Kans.

Funny how time takes care of everything. Those glaciers? Global warming is already melting them for us.

Notes

1. Upper Basin: Utah, Colorado, Wyoming, New Mexico. Lower Basin: California, Nevada, Arizona.

2. Whose name was later changed to Hualapai Canyon, perhaps to "honor" the local Hualapai tribe in the same way that Lake Powell "honors" the man whose beloved canyon Lake Powell buried.

3. Later these dams would supposedly finance a gargantuan plan to "augment" the Colorado River with water from the Columbia, except that the Northwest had different ideas, plus they've managed to ruin on their own – with 36 dams – the once greatest salmon river system in the world.

4. What also has happened is that as the population of the desert Southwest explodes and cities start running out of water, they lease it from the farmers, which facilitates more growth, which necessitates more water, which...

5. To oversimplify, the Corps of Engineers is to the eastern half of the country what the Bureau of Reclamation is to the western, and many of its projects just as mind-bogglingly mindless.

6. Ice Harbor, Lower Monumental, Little Goose, and Lower Granite.

Sources

"America's Most Endangered Rivers of 2004: #3, *Snake River.*" americanrivers.org

"Drawdown: Groundwater Mining on Black Mesa." Natural Resources Defense Council. www.nrdc.org

Fradkin, Philip. L. *A River No More.* Tucson: University of Arizona P., 1984.

Glen Canyon Institute. glencanyon.org

Hanemann, Michael. "The Central Arizona Project." *CUDARE Working Papers* (University of California, Berkeley.)

Leopold, Aldo. *A Sand County Almanac.* New York: Ballantine, 1970.

"National Inventory of Dams." U.S. Army Corps of Engineers. http://crunch.tec.army.mil/nid/webpag

Nies, Judith. "The Black Mesa Syndrome: Indian Lands, Black Gold." *Orion.* Summer 1998.

Reisner, Marc. *Cadillac Desert*. New York: Penguin, 1993.

The Saturday Evening Post. Aug. 12, 1967 and Sept. 23, 1967.

Spain, Glen, and Zeke Grader. "Ending the Era of Big Dams: Why Some Dams Must Go." The Pacific Coast Federation of Fishermen's Associations. www.pcffa.org

Fish Story

*T*he sign that announces the famous Tellico Dam is situated so far from its namesake, and the dam itself is so nondescript, that unless you know where to look, and know what you're looking *at*, your response is likely to be...

Where?

That was my response when I drove the hour and a half from where I now live in Tennessee to have a look at the famous Tellico Dam.

All you can see from the sign is a portion of the earthen dike that extends out from the dam, not the celebrity itself, and *that's* a good half mile away and off to your right. I saw it and didn't see it several times and didn't realize what it was until I'd meandered my way much closer.

Not so proud of this dam, the TVA?

It's six-tenths of a mile long (most of that the dike) and 129 feet high, with three measly spillways. A blacktop path runs the length of the earthen part to a locked gate and sternly-worded sign that discourage further advance onto the concrete part. Below is the last snippet of the Little Tennessee River while to your left sprawls Tellico "Lake," 15,560 acres of superfluous flatwater. Dozens of condemned family farms lie under that flatwater. Also Echota, 10,000-year-old ancestral home of the Cherokee. No sign of the latter, of course, but visible here and there are spectral reminders of the former – the tops of silos standing watch above the water's surface.

But it wasn't the silos that made Tellico famous, it was the fish. The silos were part of the story, but the fish *was* the story. Little fish, big dam: big news. "Tiny Fish Stops Dam" was, you may recall, the focus of practically every Tellico news story printed and broadcast in 1978. Reporters couldn't get enough, and wouldn't let go, of the obvious irony. They also couldn't see past it, or chose not to look. Tons of coverage, then nothing (American journalism at work), for in the end the story fizzled. In the end the fish didn't stop the dam.

Fame is fleeting, and so forth. Life goes on, etc. Now people walk their dogs on Tellico Dam.

○

The Tennessee River isn't "normal."

Yes, it begins that way, in the headwaters of its tributaries, the Powell, Clinch, Holston, French Broad, and Little Tennessee rivers in western Virginia and North Carolina; and it flows predictably southwestward from Knoxville[1] between the Smokey Mountains on the east and the Cumberlands on the west; but then near Chattanooga, instead of choosing the course of least resistance, as rivers are supposed to do, and dutifully continuing to follow the Cumberland escarpment, it cuts a gorge *through* the Cumberland Mountains; and instead of then resuming its southward course, as Northern Hemisphere rivers are supposed to do, after crossing Alabama it shoots straight north, plowing back through Tennessee and up through western Kentucky and emptying, not into the Mississippi but the Ohio, at about the same latitude as where it began.

It isn't your average river in one other respect also: of all the rivers in the world (yes, that's Planet Earth), none has so much of its length buried under reservoirs as the Tennessee. That, of course, would be TVA (Tennessee Valley Authority) reservoirs, and that would seem to require some explanation.

Muscle Shoals is just a town in northwestern Alabama now, but it used to be a wild 37-mile stretch of rapids on the Tennessee River that rendered steamboat passage impossible except in the highest waters of spring, and then only if you liked living dangerously. Since most people don't, and since the towns of Chattanooga and Knoxville, upriver from the rapids, wanted the Tennessee made more navigable for commerce, Muscle Shoals was long viewed as a problem.

It became a problem of another sort when it also began to be viewed as an asset. With a drop along that 37-mile stretch of 137 feet, its hydroelectric potential was huge (in fact, second only, in the eastern half of the U.S., to Niagra Falls), and the market for electricity was growing. But this was the early twentieth century and there was much disagreement – about three decades' worth – over who should do the marketing: the federal government, or privately owned utilities? Public power advocates argued that since rivers are in the public domain (a principle that has its roots in Roman law), "development" of those rivers should be the government's responsibility, for the public good. Their private power adversaries countered that, except as a lessor and regulatory agent, the government should keep its nose out of free enterprise. The public power people complained about giveaways of our natural resources to corporations. The private power people called the other side's proposals "creeping socialism." No one, by the way, questioned whether this country's rivers should be "developed." This was an age when the word conservation *meant* development.

Meanwhile, Woodrow Wilson, using powers granted him under the National Defense Act of 1916, authorized government construction at Muscle Shoals of a dam and two nitrate plants (for the production of gunpowder), and the debate was put on hold for a couple of years. But at war's end it resumed, and this time it wasn't hypothetical: the two nitrate plants (which could be converted to produce fertilizer) and the massive dam under construction [2] were the opposing sides' very tangible focus. One side insisted that federal control of these facilities be maintained, the other that they be leased to private companies. One side argued that government power rates could act as a "yardstick" against which to measure excessive private rates, the other that the federal government had no business marketing electric power at all. Both the plants and the dam sat virtually idle for years while the debate dragged on and on.

George W. Norris, senator from Nebraska and "father" of the TVA, had some dogs in this fight. A staunch opponent of what he called the "power trust" (the private utilities were virtually unregulated at this time), he had helped win the battle in 1913 over Hetch Hetchy Valley in Yosemite National Park – no, not to save it but to determine who would get to fill it up with water. The city of San Francisco had asked Congress for permission to build a reservoir in Hetch Hetchy, and the private utilities, wanting the spoils for themselves, were bitterly opposed. Also opposed, but for slightly different reasons, were "preservationists" like John Muir who had the audacity to suggest that the valley was fine the way it was. Norris convinced Congress to let San Francisco build the dam (setting a precedent that David Brower would later fight when the Bureau of Reclamation tried to build a dam in Dinosaur National Monument), and the private utilities – and Muir and Hetch Hetchy – lost.

Norris fought long and hard to keep the Muscle Shoals facilities in federal hands, sponsoring two different congressional bills that not only would have accomplished that immediate goal but also would have provided for further federal government "development" of the Tennessee River upstream. But that raised the old free-enterprise-versus-socialism specter, and two Republican [3] presidents in a row, first Coolidge and then Hoover, vetoed Norris's Congress-approved bills.

Enter the Great Depression. Enter Franklin Roosevelt.

FDR thought big, had to under the circumstances, so when as president-elect he and Senator Norris visited Wilson Dam, he not only endorsed Norris's river-development ideas but went him one (or five or six) better by later calling for "a corporation clothed with the power of Government but possessed with the flexibility and initiative of a private enterprise" that would plan "for the proper use, conservation, and development of the natural resources of the Tennessee River drainage basin and its adjoining territory for the general social and economic welfare of the Nation" in "a return to the spirit and vision of the pioneer."

That's thinking big. It's also, let's face it, thinking a tad vaguely, but whatever the words meant, they sounded good to a country badly in need of some encouragement, and so in May of 1933, just two months into Roosevelt's famous Hundred Days, Congress passed the TVA Act.

The TVA was to be a grand experiment in what FDR called "regional planning." As governor of New York, he had become fascinated with the work of city and regional planners – like his respected uncle, Frederic Delano – who sought to make cities more orderly and liveable via measures like zoning laws and building codes and hopeful blueprints for guiding future growth. "Region," to these men, didn't mean a major river's entire watershed, just a city and its environs, or areas of ruined farmland set aside for reforestation.

But "major river's entire watershed" is exactly what Roosevelt did mean in his own use of the term "region." And not only that, he envisioned TVA-like programs spreading out in all directions across the country until at some happy time in the future all of America would be "planned."

Yes, Utopia is nice to think about, but there tend to be problems with implementation.

First of all, on the scale that Roosevelt was imagining, what can the word "planning" possibly mean? Send me your answer on a postcard when you've figured it out.

Second, the Tennessee Valley "region" (remember that giant riverine "U"?), a "region" comprised at the time of about three million people, was and is – geographically, politically, economically, racially, and agriculturally – about as diverse as a "region" can get. Ergo, it isn't a region at all.

Then there's the TVA Act.

Its Preamble authorized the TVA to create a navigation and flood control system on the Tennessee River; "to provide for reforestation and the proper use of marginal lands in the Tennessee Valley; to provide for the agricultural and industrial development of said valley"; and to operate the facilities at Muscle Shoals. That would seem to be enough to keep them occupied, but then the historically much-discussed Sections 22 and 23 of the Act (the entire document runs to 33 turbid pages) gave the nod to Roosevelt's "planning" chimera by referring vaguely to the preparation of surveys and reports whose "general purpose" would be for "fostering an orderly and proper physical, economic, and social development" of the Valley, and for ensuring "the economic and social well being of the people living in said river basin."

What all this boils down to is, as many historians have pointed out, a divided – hence ambiguous – mission. On the one hand, the TVA is told to build dams for navigation and flood control, to teach farmers in the area about crop rotation and erosion control, and to manufacture fertilizer – all concrete (and in the case of dams, very concrete) objectives. On the other, there's this abstract gobbledygook about planning for the "well being" of the Valley's people. Moreover, the Act doesn't assign priorities to the different facets of TVA's "mission" (what's more important: river navigation or soil conservation?), and it doesn't address the inevitability of conflicts between those facets – for example, between restoring farmland and drowning it under reservoirs.

But wait a minute. What happened to electricity? Wasn't the primacy of public power over private power Senator Norris's hobby horse? Isn't "rural electrification" the thing that every sixth-grader learns was TVA's big achievement? Bringing lightbulbs and the Grand Ole Opry to all those tobacco-chewing, corncob-pipe-smoking backwoods agrarians? Then where is it in the Act?

Well, it turns out that the noble TVA Act was the bastard child of congressional politics after all.

FDR may have been dreaming of an industrial Arcadia in Hillbillyland, but Norris hadn't lost sight of his long-sought goal: federal control over the hydroelectric potential of that great big Tennessee River. The problem was, a) the private utilities and their champions in Congress and, b) the Constitution: no one knew if federally marketed power was even legal. Norris's solution was to foreground what was safe – navigation and flood control, over which the government clearly did have jurisdiction – and push back into the shadows of his bill what was not: electric power. Power, the bill claimed, would just be the by-product, the "Oh yes, that too," of dams built primarily for the first two purposes. This ploy fooled no one, least of all the private utilities – who kept TVA in court for the next decade defending itself against the charge that it was really just a big, specially-favored power company with a multi-purpose "mission" as a cover – but this time Norris had his ace in the hole: the president.

So. Vague, ill-defined, divided, ambiguous, convoluted, and downright confusing or not, TVA's "mission" was laid out (sort of).

And not surprisingly, there were problems:

. . . There were problems between the first presidentially-appointed three-member board of directors, one of whom (Arthur E. Morgan) had been bitten by Roosevelt's quixotic planning bug, another (David Lilienthal) who wanted none of *that* and felt that TVA's focus should be cheap electric power for the Valley's benighted residents, and a third (Harcourt A. Morgan – no relation to Arthur) who, as an agriculturist, was clearly the most environmentally sensitive of the three but who sided with Lilienthal against the first Morgan because of the first Morgan's autocratic tendencies, which led to bitter – and very public – infighting, which led to Roosevelt's eventual dismissal of Morgan one.

. . . There were those problems in the courts.

. . . And there were problems just trying to figure out how to proceed.

But proceed they did, and with a vengeance, building sixteen dams by 1945, permanently flooding hundreds of thousands of acres of land (need I point out the irony?), and transforming the Tennessee River into a 652-mile-long series of slackwater pools.

TVA built 49 dams in all, the last of which was Tellico. Norris Dam, at the confluence of the Clinch and Powell rivers, just north of Knoxville, was the first.

Wilson Dam (which had been built by the Army Corps of Engineers but was subsequently turned over to TVA) had successfully annihilated Muscle Shoals, making that 37-mile stretch of the river navigable, but the Tennessee's uneven seasonal flows necessitated the creation of "storage" reservoirs on its tributaries to produce a dependably navigable river year-round. Norris Dam, named of course for our senator, was built for that reason, as well as (oh, yes) power.

Board-of-directors bickering, legal briar thickets, and "How do we get this going?" weren't the only problems. There was also the problem (to put it gently) of "population removal" – i.e. (to put it less gently) of kicking people out of their homes and off their land. In the case of Norris Dam, this meant that 3,500 families (not people: families) had to be moved.

TVA took (by buying, at what most people agreed was a fair enough price) 153,000 acres of land for the Norris project, almost 59% of which would *not* be covered by water. Why? Because the "planners" in the agency wanted to plan – for industry, recreation, and the retirement of marginal land. Also, since much of the farmland in the area *was* marginal and therefore subject to erosion, TVA didn't want their reservoirs silting up. Reforestation (not, in this case, education and restoration) would help to slow that inevitable process down. [4]

But much of East Tennessee was, by rural standards, already densely settled (farms being divided and then divided again through inheritance) and as a result the land already stressed, so where are all these people going to go when the amount of land available to them has been reduced by 153,000 acres?

Answer? God maybe knows, but not the TVA.

There was no relocation plan at all in the first year of land purchases (as the dam was quickly going up). After that, the plan consisted of little more than giving advice to the dispossessed about available real estate. Advice, that is, if they could afford to buy what was for sale, and many of the small landowners – the largest group – could not, because with so much land gobbled up by the TVA, land prices rose (at the same time that the tax base for the affected counties shrunk). Since most people chose to stay in the reservoir area (which, after all, was their home, often extending back for generations), many ended up with smaller farms on poorer land than they'd had before. TVA had given them a "fair" price for their farms, but no additional compensation for the rising market, for the trauma of being uprooted, or for the cost and inconvenience of relocation – and no compensation whatsoever for the tenant farmers, who comprised a full one-third of those "removed."

Remember "fostering...the economic and social well being of the people living in said river basin"?

A few people resisted, but not many (rising waters make for a rather convincing argument), and those who did were given a free lesson on the legal particulars of eminent domain. TVA had *worsened* the area's problems of rural overpopulation, but instead of learning from its mistakes, doggedly kept repeating them until, by 1946, more than 14,000 families had been removed from sixteen different reservoir sites (Davidson 255). Ironically (if "ironically" even covers it), TVA *did not even want to build* some of those dams, for there was no market for the electricity, but was forced to build them by the navigation ruse in the TVA Act, a ruse that probably did result in "fostering the economic well being" of several shipping companies, but not the downtrodden Depression-era people of the Tennessee Valley (Chandler 37).

○

Tellico Dam was TVA's attempt to revitalize its ill-conceived mission. If anyone had doubts prior to World War II that the agency was anything more than a big power company, the war laid those doubts to rest. To its credit, TVA threw everything it had into the war effort, converting its fertilizer program into nitrates production for explosives, supplying most of the power needed by the Maryville, Tennessee, ALCOA company, which had furiously stepped up its production of aluminum for the manufacture of airplanes, and powering that very power-hungry top secret program underway at Oakridge. But by war's end, the grand experiment in regional planning, which had barely gotten off the ground to begin with, was a dead duck. TVA's habitual justification for its existence – navigation, flood control, and (oh, yes) power – wasn't a plan for much of anything but building dams. Making the Tennessee River navigable for barge traffic certainly hadn't "saved" the region (currently, less than one barge per day makes it to Knoxville) (Ferrar 1); flood control on the river was mostly for the benefit of the industrial section of one city, Chattanooga, which was built – guess where? – on a flood plain (over 243,000 acres upstream of Chattanooga permanently buried under water to protect 8,760 acres downstream) (Chandler 78)[5]; and hydroelectric power hadn't magically transformed the Tennessee Valley into a land of economic prosperity: rural electrification, industrial development, and per capita income progressed more *slowly* in the TVA states [6] than in economically similar surrounding areas (Chandler 43-63).

Nevertheless!

The myth (TVA historians use the word "myth" rather frequently) that TVA brought unprecedented economic growth to the Tennessee Valley, that it singlehandedly "uplifted" an entire poverty-stricken region, took hold, and persisted, and persists to this day. So at the end of World War II, when it looked as if TVA's "mission" had degenerated into just cranking out lots of electricity, much of it not even for the Valley but for the federal government, and when the main stem of the Tennessee River had already been dammed to the hilt, TVA's leaders (who nurtured, and may have even believed in, the myth themselves) began looking around for a new "mission," and the river's tributaries, starting with the Little Tennessee, which tumbles out of North Carolina and joins the bigger stream at Lenoir City, Tennessee, is where their gazes fell.

○

Tellico was first proposed in 1936, as an "extension" of the nearby Fort Loudoun Dam (you can see the larger dam from the smaller one; two huge TVA reservoirs practically within shouting distance of each other), but by 1945 was listed, by the TVA itself, as next-to-last out of 22 "non-urgent" projects (Wheeler and McDonald 30)[7]. However, in 1959, partly because, at the outset, it had a better perceived benefit-cost ratio than other similar projects, partly because it had just been on the books, unbuilt, for so long, Tellico was selected to lead the Tennessee Valley Authority triumphantly into the future. "Regional planning" returned – dressed this time a little more modestly, but otherwise not appreciably changed: dams would create reservoirs, reservoirs would attract industry, and presto! another uplifted region. Just *why* reservoirs were supposed to attract industry – what's the attraction? – is a question no one ever asked. "Miniature TVAs in the tributaries!" was the call to action. "Factories in the fields!" was the stirring vision (Wheeler and McDonald 19).

But you don't repeatedly kick people off their land and out of their homes, repeatedly drown farmland, repeatedly bury rivers, without eventually someone taking notice. Also, in the three decades following World War II, TVA drew less than favorable notice in other ways. Its coal-fired steam plants, the first of which was built in the early forties (there are now thirteen), were using prodigious amounts of eastern Kentucky coal, and eastern Kentucky was being strip-mined into oblivion as a result. These same plants were far out of compliance with both federal and state sulfur dioxide emissions standards, but instead of complying with the standards TVA fought the Environmental Protection Agency for years. Finally in 1977, after amendments were made to the Clean Air Act that require federal agencies to abide by state emissions laws; after law suits were filed against TVA by a coalition of groups including the Sierra Club, the Alabama Lung Association, the Tennessee League of Women Voters, Save Our Cumberland Mountains, and the National Resources Defense Council; and after similar suits were filed by the states of Alabama and Kentucky, TVA was forced to stop acting like it was the only game in town...but it remains one of the nation's biggest polluters to this day.

(Why those coal-fired steam plants and not more dams? Because most of the hydroelectric sites were already dammed. Tellico was not a hydro project.)

So TVA was carrying some baggage by the time people in the lower Little Tennessee River valley became fully aware of the agency's plans to build Tellico Dam. And that took a few years because TVA was at first disingenuously noncommittal about those plans, and then deliberately misleading about, a) the amount of land it intended to take and, b) Tellico's economic viability. After the 1930s and the imaginary heyday of regional planning, TVA ended its policy of purchasing far more land than its reservoirs would cover (e.g. more than double the amount that Norris Reservoir covers) and began transferring the acquired surplus to other public agencies, and reselling it to private parties and land developers [8]. A "small" purchase policy replaced its "heavy" purchase predecessor as TVA's "multi-purpose" mission became "unified," as it were, around kilowatts. But the "new" mission, which Tellico was intended to exemplify, required a return to the heavy purchase policy so that land would be available, once the reservoir was filled, for all those lakeshore industries that would then materialize with syllogistic certitude. 39,000 acres were, in fact, bought up (or condemned when the ingrates wouldn't cooperate) for a reservoir whose maximum capacity is 16,500 acres. Much of the extra land was then to be resold...but not because the original idyllic "plan" for it had not worked out, and not just as a way for TVA to recoup its costs, but because buying-to-resell – at a hefty profit – *was* the plan.

This was not news that TVA was eager to make public. First of all, buying-to-resell, at a profit or no profit, was controversial, and perhaps illegal, in itself. Who was TVA to decide that Farmer Jones's farm was less important than Company X's product? What right did TVA have to take someone's land and then give it to someone else? Second (and this was where the shaky ground began to pitch and roll), TVA was not, for whatever reason, *choosing* to resell the surplus land. It *had* to resell that land, and for one reason only: the dam whose whole purpose was economic rejuvenation made no economic sense.

TVA's traditional justification for its dams – navigation, flood control, ohyespower – just didn't fly with Tellico. Navigation? A mere 33 miles' worth (the length of the reservoir). Barge "traffic" on Tellico is nonexistent. Flood control? Marginal and debatable at best. Power? Tellico doesn't even have generators of its own; instead, it "boosts," via a canal, the output of nextdoor-neighbor Fort Loudoun Dam by about one-fourth of Fort

Loudoun's capacity [9]. Even TVA's top dog at the time, Aubrey J. Wagner, admitted, during a foot-in-the-mouth moment, that Tellico's contribution in these areas would be "relatively insignificant" (Hargrove and Conkin 183), and TVA never seriously argued for Tellico on traditional grounds.

But Congress requires (at least in theory, if not in porcine practice) that the projected benefits of any publicly-financed project outweigh its costs, meaning a "benefit-cost ratio" of at least 1.1 to 1.0, and so "new methods of economic justification," to use Wagner's own words, had to be found (Hargrove and Conkin 177).

But what?

It is a measure of just how bad a project Tellico was that even though this was only (wink, wink) a "numbers game," TVA struggled for over five years to come up with a barely acceptable benefit-cost ratio of 1.4 to 1.0. To arrive at this figure, mathematical legerdemain of a truly impressive character was employed. First, TVA added three new sources of benefits to the original trinity: land "enhancement" (i.e. resale), recreation, and "general economic benefits" (industrial development). Then, according to historians William Bruce Wheeler and Michael J. McDonald in their book *TVA and the Tellico Dam*, it made five bogus assumptions:

✓. . . Without the dam, no economic progress in the region would occur at all.

✓. . . With the dam, all economic progress that did occur in the region was the dam's doing.

✓. . . Whatever form of bounty Tellico could bring to the region it would.

✓. . . Tellico would not undermine economic benefits already in place but would only augment them.

✓. . . Costs of the Tellico project would not rise (no guffaws, please) beyond the then-current rate of inflation (92-93).

To make land enhancement work, i.e. to make it lucrative enough to benefit the benefits column, TVA "calculated" land values, not a year or two into the future but decades into the future, using highly conjectural econometric models especially designed, one could say, for the occasion. These models conveniently failed to subtract inflation-related increases in land values, instead attributing all land-value increases to the project. And to make matters better, since adjoining land not held by TVA might, just by virtue of its proximity to the project, rise in value as well, those "enhancements" were also counted *even though TVA did not own that land* (Wheeler and McDonald 90, 43, 94).

Calculating recreation benefits would require...perhaps a little more tweaking of the numbers. But first, of course, numbers had to be found. How to estimate the number of visitors per year that Tellico would attract, and the amount of money each would spend? Especially when most of those visitors would probably be locals who would not spend much at all? And especially when 22 artificial lakes, 16 of them TVA's, were already available within a 50-mile radius? (Fact: Tennessee has more shoreline than all the Great Lakes combined.) And especially when recreational opportunities of a much rarer and potentially more profitable order already existed on the Little Tennessee river, to wit, excellent trout fishing and fast-water canoeing on one of the last remaining lowland trout streams in that whole part of the country?

How? Well, you find yourself a hat, throw some numbers into it, pull a number out, and then instead of deducting from that number the amount of money that the estimated 24,000 trout fishermen per year currently spend in the area, *you leave the fishermen in* even though, once your reservoir is filled, those trout fishermen's trout stream will be history (Wheeler and McDonald 97, 99).

After land enhancement and recreation, "general economic benefits" was easy: assume all 5,000 acres of available shoreline will be snatched up by industry; assume all these industries will be barge-dependent upon the coal, stone, sand, and gravel that barges most commonly transport, thus increasing your navigation benefit; assume all the agricultural workers whose jobs will be lost along with the land will not be replaced by industrial workers from outside but will happily flock to the factories; completely ignore the $4 million in farm income that will be lost every year when those 39,000 acres of prime farmland [10] are flooded or "enhanced"; ignore those within your own agency who cling to the quaint notion that preserving farmland is good; and your case is made (Wheeler and McDonald 99-104).

Not surprisingly, however, TVA was in no great hurry to make this case in the light of day, which handicapped the dam's early opponents (chiefly farmers, anglers, and other outdoors enthusiasts), who were not even sure how much land TVA intended to take until 1967, the year construction began. But by 1971, with costs (surprise, surprise) rising, congressional appropriations (expensive war being waged) shrinking, construction consequently slowing, and most importantly, a national environmental movement emerging, things began to change. Unable to get their hands on

TVA's potentially project-busting benefit-cost connivings, the opposition focused on what it could: the peaceful valley and its beautiful river that the dam would destroy. Headline-grabbing Supreme Court Justice William O. Douglas pointedly visited the area in 1969 to do some trout fishing, then published an article in *True* magazine entitled "This Valley Waits to Die" that, temporarily, got the nation's attention. That same year Congress passed the National Environmental Policy Act (NEPA) with its "Environmental Impact Statement" (EIS) requirement, which first had TVA insisting that since the Tellico project predated the Act it didn't apply, then grudgingly drawing up a "draft statement," then landing in court when the Environmental Defense Fund sued the agency on the grounds that, a) it hadn't formally filed an EIS and, b) the draft statement was a joke. A U.S. District Court judge issued a swift and stunning (to TVA) restraining order against the agency that stopped construction on the dam for the better part of two years.

But the injunction was eventually lifted, and Justice Douglas's article soon faded from the nation's frail memory, and Tellico ceased to be news except to a small band of Davids flinging stones at Goliath. An obscure dam in Somewhere, Tennessee, couldn't hope to compete for the nation's attention with the war in Vietnam and the burgeoning Watergate scandal and the protest movement *du jour*.

Until the fish.

○

It was both fortuitous and risky.

On August 12, 1973 David Etnier, a University of Tennessee biology professor and ichthyologist who had testified in the Environmental Defense Fund suit that the reservoir would likely destroy two species of fish already listed as endangered, was snorkeling about seven miles above the dam when he spied a 3-inch perch-like fish that he'd never before seen. Prudent scientist that he was, Etnier mostly kept quiet about his find while conducting more research on the fish, but was soon convinced he'd discovered a new species – which he named "snail darter," for its penchant for escargot – and one that could be classified as endangered.

The opposition, by now, was on the ropes. Their best argument – TVA's trumped-up, math-defying shell game of a benefit-cost ratio – was unprovable thanks to TVA's mystery-shrouded bookkeeping. Buying-to-resell looked unethical, if not illegal, on its face, but the courts had never questioned what a federal agency concluded was the "public good." Three hundred fifty families were being displaced by the project, but the larger public was largely indifferent to what was happening. And though the imminent watery destruction of ancient Cherokee village and burial sites had much news-making potential, the Cherokee's Eastern Band, for whatever their own reasons (general white-man suspicion?), couldn't be persuaded to join the fight. [11]

So the fish was a lucky break, as was that same year's Endangered Species Act (ESA) which, unlike two earlier versions, had some teeth: enforcement was placed in the hands of the federal courts, and private citizens could sue non-complying federal agencies. But it was also the only weapon the opposition had, and not only was it *just* a fish, and a small and modestly-named one at that (instead of, say a "Freedom Eagle" or a "Liberty Moose"), it was likely to be seen by the public as a zoological manifestation of that much-derided phenomenon, The Technicality. Would arguing that construction on a (nearly completed) dam be stopped to save a three-inch fish no one had ever heard of make a travesty of their cause? Would even some of their supporters recoil from such a "cynical" strategy? And would the end result be a backlash against environmental causes in general? Would their cause harm the larger cause? Might they and their comrades-in-arms be perceived – in the eyes of the ignorant masses, and with the aid of the sensationalist Press – as "radicals" and "extremists"?

But...the snail darter was the only weapon they had. As old and obdurate holdout-landowner Asa McCall put it at an October 1974 meeting of the extremists: "I've never heard of this little fish, but if it can save our farms, I say let's give it a try" (Plater "Law and" 7).

And try they did. Zygmunt ("Zyg") Plater, who had been hired the year before as a new assistant professor by the University of Tennessee College of Law, and who had quickly become active in the Tellico fight, threw all his youthful energy into getting the fish placed on the Endangered Species List, into forcing TVA to stop construction on the dam while the fish was swimming its way through the requisite paperwork, and once its endangered status was achieved, into forcing TVA to stop construction while the Little Tennessee River was being considered as the fish's "critical habitat," since no one could find the fish anywhere else.[12] Both construction injunctions failed, but when the river's critical-habitat status was also achieved, Plater and company tried again, failed again, appealed to the Sixth Circuit Court of Appeals in Cincinnati, and this time won. The judge's ruling on January

31, 1977 was that unless Congress specifically exempted Tellico from the Endangered Species Act, the dam was toast.

TVA's reaction – besides appealing to the Supreme Court, begging Congress to exempt Tellico from the ESA, and halting construction on the dam itself but not on other dam-related aspects of the project – was to ask the U.S. Fish and Wildlife Service, which oversees the ESA, to "delist" the Little Tennessee River as the snail darter's critical habitat on the grounds, in effect, that TVA had already ruined it. Fish and Wildlife demurred.

With the Supreme Court showdown looming, Congress's General Accounting Office issued a report on Tellico that blasted TVA's economic hocus-pocus and recommended to Congress that no more money be spent on the project until the agency could produce a more viable benefit-cost ratio. Fully practiced in the art of absurd maneuverings by now, TVA's response was to produce a *less* viable benefit-cost ratio of 7 to 1 by balancing Tellico's fanciful benefits against the costs that *remained* instead of the project's total costs (Wheeler and McDonald 200).

The Supreme Court's six-to-three ruling against TVA on June 15, 1978, and the "Silly Little Fish Stops Big Important Dam" headlines that instantly followed are probably what you remember from the snail darter story if you remember it at all. Plater and his team had taken great pains to lay out for the Court all the ways in which Tellico was a pork barrel boondoggle of the first order, and all the eminently more sensible alternatives to the dam, but Chief Justice Warren Burger, who wrote the majority opinion, focused only on whether or not the courts could take it upon themselves to interpret Congress's intent in passing the Endangered Species Act (warm and fuzzy protected, cold and clammy no?) and concluded they could not. It was a narrowly defined victory but a victory nonetheless, and Plater, who three years earlier had been denied tenure by his UT Law School colleagues (everything aboveboard, of course, except that anyone who has been a part of academia knows that boat-rocking isn't esteemed), had perhaps the additional pleasure of imagining his detractors turning a sickly green as their spurned colleague argued before the Supreme Court what legal scholars now generally regard as the most important environmental protection case ever.

But the Court's ruling did not of course please TVA, nor the dam's boosters, prominent among whom was powerful Tennessee senator Howard Baker, who had vowed to work to amend the Endangered Species Act and make it "reasonable" if the Court didn't rule against cold and clammies. The amendment he secured created the Endangered Species Committee (soon dubbed the "God Squad"), a seven-member board of cabinet-level administration officials whose task it would be to make an exception to the ESA when a federal project under review was deemed more important than the species the federal project would rub out. The obvious assumption was that a "reasonable" group of high-level political appointees would – as Baker later fumed, protesting the outcome – "apply common sense and just override the injunction" (Plater "The Snail").

But the senator's scheme backfired. On January 23, 1979, after holding hearings on Tellico in both Knoxville and Washington, and without even mentioning the fish, the board voted unanimously to let the injunction stand. Said board member Charles Schultze, then chairman of the Council of Economic Advisors: "Here is a project that is 95% complete, and if one takes just the cost of finishing it against the total benefits, and does it properly, it doesn't pay – which says something about the original design." Later, board chair and Secretary of the Interior Cecil Andrus added: "Frankly, I hate to see the snail darter get the credit for stopping a project that was so ill-conceived and uneconomical in the first place" (Wheeler and McDonald 211).

In a just world, i.e. one without a U.S. Congress, that would have been the end of it. But Baker wasn't finished. With the public still convinced, thanks to shallow coverage in the Press, that the issue was those crazy fish-hugging environmentalists (the God Squad story was carried on page 12 in the *Washington Post*, page 21 in the *New York Times*, and similarly obscurely, if at all, everywhere else, whereas "Fish Stops Dam" had been front-page), one of Baker's cronies in the House of Representatives, John Duncan of "Tellico District," Tennessee, pulled off one of the dirtiest political tricks ever engineered, even for Congress. On a dull afternoon in the House in June of 1979, the chambers practically empty, as a clerk was plodding verbally through the minutia of the 1980 public works appropriations bill, Duncan came forward with an amendment that he claimed was uncontroversial, moved that for that reason it need not even be read, was supported in this naked lie by two pork-fed members of the House Appropriations Committee – who just happened to be in attendance – and in less than a minute, by a voice vote from a handful of oblivious fools, Tellico was exempted from the Endangered Species Act. Baker then strong-armed the rider through the Senate, President Carter cravenly backed off from a veto, and on November 29, 1979 the waters of Tellico "Lake" began to rise.

O

On the mild December morning that I visited the lake, the water was still, inviolate-looking, and sky-reflection blue. In the distance a lone fisherman stood fishing from his skiff, and the only sounds were the hiss of traffic on the state highway a half-mile to the west and the rattle of a kingfisher over the water.

As I stood there on the dam reviewing what I'd learned about the postscript to our story – that the handful of companies TVA had managed to coax to Tellico's shores employs, twenty-six years after impoundment, about 3,000 people (www.tellico.com), hardly the 25,000 TVA had grandiously predicted; that the land for which TVA paid those it evicted an average of $450 per acre is now selling for $200,000 to $750,000 per unimproved *lot* in the posh country-club, yacht-club, equestrian-club "planned communities" of Tellico Village and Rarity Bay; that a 2004 EPA-approved Tennessee Department of Environment and Conservation report calls Tellico's water "impaired" because of PCB contamination (don't eat the catfish); and that TVA's own "ecological health rating" for Tellico (too much chlorophyll, not enough oxygen, and don't expect much from the fishing) is "poor" – as I reflected upon these things, I looked out over the water trying to imagine the Little Tennessee River valley as it once had been, and could not. I'd seen pictures, of course, but the lake was here and the valley was not, and I was used to it almost as soon as I first laid eyes on it. Who can stay angry forever? The valley that is now a reservoir, the forest that is now a subdivision, the pasture that is now a parking lot – you just get used to it. You either remember the way it was, or you don't, but in time no one remembers the way it was, no one feels the loss, and then the next tree is felled, the next pasture paved.

Ahead of me on the blacktop path was a killdeer keeping its distance, quick-walking to preserve that distance, then stopping whenever I stopped. As I watched it, nine honking Canada geese and something white flew in from the south and alighted on the water's surface. The white, my binoculars informed me, was a ring-billed gull, a fairly common winter visitor to Tennessee but not that I'd ever seen in company with geese.

I resumed my walk. The killdeer took flight with a shrill *ki-deee, ki-deee, ki-deee!* A meadowlark began singing off to my right. When I looked back at the lake, the gull was still there, floating placidly amongst the geese. It didn't seem to know it didn't belong.

Notes

1. The confluence of the Holston and French Broad rivers just east of Knoxville is the Tennessee's "official," i.e. politically designated, beginning.

2. Eventually to be called Wilson Dam. It wasn't completed until 1925.

3. Norris was himself a Republican, but proudly called himself "the fighting liberal." These were different times...

4. The agriculturalists in the agency were opposed, for obvious reasons, to this "heavy purchase" policy, but the agriculturalists didn't have much say.

5. All in all, TVA flooded under its reservoirs more land – three quarters of a million acres – than a flood so rare it will theoretically occur only once in every 500 years (Chandler 78-79).

6. Chiefly Tennessee, Mississippi, Alabama, and Kentucky.

7. Its purpose as an extension of Fort Loudoun, via a (short) canal between the two reservoirs, was to enhance (marginally – some would say negligibly) Fort Loudoun's navigation, flood control, and power capabilities.

8. 171,000 and 147,000 acres respectively by 1960 (Wheeler and McDonald 11).

9. If that sounds significant, consider this: Today, TVA – the nation's largest public utility – generates 60% of its power from its coal-fired steam plants, 30% from its nuclear plants, and only 10% from *all* 49 of its dams. I tried calculating Tellico's infinitesimal percentage, but my calculator dove inside itself for the answer and never returned.

10. The lower Little Tennessee River valley was an anomaly for hardscrabble East Tennessee, and practically everywhere else. Because of its wide and shallow geography, it contained some of the richest farmland *in the world*, with topsoil an astounding 16 feet deep.

11. They finally did announce their opposition to the dam in 1977, after the snail darter had already grabbed the limelight.

12. Years later, small populations of the snail darter were found in a few other streams, and its status is now threatened instead of endangered.

Sources

Chandler, William U. *The Myth of TVA: Conservation and Development in the Tennessee Valley, 1933-1983*. Cambridge, MA: Ballinger Publishing Company, 1984.

Davidson, Donald. *The Tennessee, Volume Two – The New River: Civil War to TVA*. Nashville, TN: J.S. Sanders and Company, 1948, 1992.

Hargrove, Erwin C. *Prisoners of Myth: The Leadership of the Tennessee Valley Authority, 1933-1990*. Princeton, NJ: Princeton University Press, 1994.

Hargrove, Erwin C. and Paul K. Conkin, eds. *TVA: Fifty years of Grass-Roots Bureaucracy*. Urbana, IL: University of Illinois Press, 1983.

McDonald, Michael J. and John Muldowny. *TVA and the Dispossessed: The Resettlement of Population in the Norris Dam Area*. Knoxville, TN: The University of Tennessee Press, 1982.

Neely, Jack. "Tellico Dam Revisited." *Metro Pulse*. 9 Dec. 2004: 1-14 (online pages).

Plater, Zygmunt J.B. "Law and the Fourth Estate: Endangered Nature, the Press, and the Dicey Game of Democratic Governance." *Environmental Law* 32 (Winter 2002): 1-36.

—. "The Snail Darter, the Tellico Dam, and Sustainable Democracy Lessons for the Next President from a Classic Environmental Law Controversy." Boston College of Law School Lectures and Presentations. (Internet source.)

Tellico Reservoir Development Agency. www.tellico.com

Wheeler, William Bruce and Michael J. McDonald. *TVA and the Tellico Dam: 1936-1979*. Knoxville, TN: The University of Tennessee Press, 1986.

TWO:

THE BIRDS
AND THE BUNYANS

Out of the Air

*T*his spring I'm trying to learn birdsong. Last spring, for my birthday, my wife gave me the Peterson Field Guides tapes *Birding By Ear*, three cassettes containing the songs of eighty-five species, and it's taken me a year to get birdsong-serious. The tapes are time- and concentration-consuming both – you have to listen to them often, and closely, to make any progress – and I just hadn't yet reached that level of interest. I sat down to them several times with good intentions, learned a few songs, promptly forgot them during those periods when I wasn't playing the tapes, and finally filed them away in my mind under "Someday."

But spring has that habit of always returning, and returning with it this time was *I want to learn those songs*. Why the italicized interest now and not the year before, or even why the interest at all, I'm not sure. I'd lived my entire life – fast approaching half a century – in blissful ignorance of all but the handful of songs that everyone knows; why had that ignorance suddenly begun to nag? Pleasant evenings sitting on the deck listening vaguely to the sprinklings of avian music all around were now disrupted by "Damn it, what bird was that?"

In a sense it's pointless knowledge – putting a name to a sound coming from a tree. Once you've "named" the sound, there isn't much to do but name another...and another...until you return to "Damn it, what bird was that?" The sound doesn't know or care that you've named it, doesn't know it has a name, sounds just fine to itself without one. "That's an indigo bunting... That's a titmouse...Hey, a wood thrush!" ("That's a human," quoth the bird, "with nothing to do.")

On the other hand – since visual or aural access to birds is simply a matter of looking out the window or stepping outside, since birds are even more broadly dispersed on the planet than human beings, since they're everywhere we turn, whether we're standing in a virgin forest or on a noisy city street – it's something close to astonishing that most of us *can't* put names to the songs and calls of the birds in our own backyards. No bird on this continent is more widely recognized than the American robin – it's probably the first bird every child learns – and yet until recently I'd have been hard-pressed to identify its bouncy song, much less its whinny call or its bright, emphatic *teep*! I knew the *caw* of the American crow and the house sparrow's monotonous bark (though I called the latter just "sparrow," not knowing that there are many species of sparrow nor that the house sparrow is an import and not a sparrow but a finch); I knew *bob-WHITE* and *WHIP-poor-WILL* only because they so plainly say their names; I knew the northern mockingbird only because it sings so many songs (undoubtedly confusing it part of the time with the even more talented brown thrasher, of whose existence I was ignorant); and having grown up in Kansas, I knew the lilting *SPRING-of-THE-year* of the eastern meadowlark. Blue jay, northern cardinal, European starling – perhaps I "knew" some of these common birds' many vocalizations when I saw them vocalizing, but could not have picked their sounds out of the air. And the equally common song sparrow, killdeer, chimney swift, eastern towhee, house finch, common grackle, Carolina wren...no clue.

The problem, of course, is that we do often have to pick their sounds out of the air; most birdsong you're hearing at any given moment is disembodied. Now that I *can* distinguish between a mockingbird and a brown thrasher (the mockingbird repeats each song several times, the burrier-sounding brown thrasher only twice), I hear both of them frequently in my neighborhood, but though mockingbirds, with their penchant for singing from the highest possible perch, are easy to spot, brown thrashers tend to be more secretive. Most singing birds are either nearby but hidden, or so far away their distance hides them from view.

Also, especially in the early morning when everybody's sounding off at once (the "dawn chorus," it's called – atmospherically, the best time for song transmission), there is such a jumbled profusion of birdsong – layer upon layer of competing melodies – that you wonder how you'll ever sort it all out. Add to that the fact that all birds have a repertoire of shorter, less melodic calls (which are used for such purposes as flock contact and food and predator location) as well as songs, that the character of a song can vary from bird to bird within a single species and from song to song within a single bird, and that some species' songs sound distressingly similar – and you wonder how the *birds* can sort it all out.

They can, though, and that's the whole purpose of birdsong: communication. Birds can no more see through a dense screen of leaves than can humans, so song has evolved as a way of transmitting information to both companions and competitors of the same species. They don't listen to the songs of other species; in a room full of people speaking different languages, you talk with those who speak the language you know. If you're a songbird in the springtime, you're mostly telling males of your own species to keep off the territory you've established, and inviting females to come check out your new lodgings. Later, after you've found yourself a wife and are raising a family, you're still sending out warnings to the leftover bachelors, and agreeing with your neighbors that Robert Frost had it right about good fences. You're also telling your wife how much you love her so that she won't succumb to the crooning of anyone else.

Those are the two primary functions of birdsong: establishing and maintaining a territory, and establishing and maintaining a bond with a female. Males in the spring on the claims they've staked sing the most, though the females of some species (e.g. song sparrow, northern cardinal) also sing; some birds (northern cardinal, Carolina wren) sing year-round, though not as much; and many birds sing, perhaps as a form of rehearsal, during spring migration. Testosterone levels govern the amount of singing: when those levels rise in the spring (triggered by the increase in daylight), singing commences or intensifies, and when they drop several months later, it tapers off or ceases altogether. Birds *can* sing after that (and some occasionally do) – they're just not "aroused" enough to sing. The old romantic notion that birds make music because they're "happy" may not be correct, but they aren't exactly singing the blues either.

Female arousal also figures in birdsong. Male singing stimulates not only female interest but, ornithologists have discovered, ovulation – and even the desire to mate. (Wine not required; just the sweet music.) And females *choose* their mates – instead of putting out for just any warbling cad – both on the basis of quantity and quality of song. Males who sing the most and with more variability are chosen over their less talented rivals perhaps because more time spent singing indicates less time required for feeding, which indicates better territory, which indicates "better" male who was able to secure that territory, which ensures greater reproductive success for the female through better quality offspring – the "good genes" model of sexual selection. But that's only "perhaps." Quantity of singing does seem to fit that model, but why some species have developed such extraordinarily complex songs and/or such complex repertoires of song, while other species haven't, still has ornithologists scratching their heads.

That complexity, both in struggling my way through it as a listener and in reading about it (my principle source is *Bird Song* by Catchpole and Slater, Cambridge U. Press, 1995; it is a survey of, if I counted correctly, 676 other sources on the subject), is to me one of the most fascinating aspects of birdsong. It's made physiologically possible, first of all, by the bird's syrinx, which, unlike a human's larynx, enables the bird to produce two sets of sounds at once. The house wren's tumbling cascade of bubbly notes, the bobolink's seemingly chaotic swirl of phrases, the veery's downwardly spiraling self-harmony – nope, we can't do that. We also can't hear nearly as acutely as birds; they are capable of a far more accurate separation of sounds. When recorded and slowed down or when visually transposed by a device called a sonograph, songs invariably reveal themselves to contain many more notes than we can hear at normal speed – the reason one robin may sound very much like every other to us, but not, of course, to the robins. Birds also possess what I've already mentioned as song "repertoires." Many species sing more than one version of their song – notes dropped, notes added, notes rearranged or re-inflected – and the collection of these versions is called the bird's repertoire. The different song versions are not accidents ("Oops, forgot a note there") but structured changes, and the sizes of some species' repertoires would put many an opera singer to shame. Those lowly starlings schlepping around in your backyard? 21 to 67. That mockingbird popping off on top of the telephone pole? 53 to 150. And the mockingbird's shy comrade-in-mimicry, the brown thrasher? They gave up counting at 2000.

Song repertoires apparently serve the same two purposes as song in general: to attract females (yes, the ladies prefer the bigger ones) and repel competing males. One theory about the latter is that large repertoires make it appear to other males that the area is already occupied, thus discouraging encroachment that much more readily. My own theory about the former, jokes aside, is that birds do on some level "enjoy" their singing, that it isn't all just territory and genes, that there is an aesthetic component to birdsong, not just for humans, but for birds as well. Ornithologists are of course loath to engage in such speculation, but Catchpole and Slater do offer as one explanation of birdsong complexity the female's "sensory bias," which sounds pretty close to "aesthetic taste" to me.

Postulating some sort of rudimentary aesthetic sensibility for birds is really only one step beyond what ornithologists now state unequivocally: that songbirds do not simply "inherit" their songs, the way they inherit the color of their plumage – they learn them. How and when they learn, from whom they learn, and the degree to which they learn all vary with each species, but the conclusion is clear: what you're hearing isn't the twitterings of a little robot. Many species learn their songs months before they themselves begin to sing; months later what they memorized streams forth. For most there is an early period of jumbled phrasings called "sub-song," followed by a closer approximation of "full song" called "plastic song," but come spring – somehow – everyone knows their parts. Some birds learn from their fathers, some from their territorial neighbors, probably most from a combination of the two. Most birds stop learning after the first year, but some can learn later than that, and a few – notably the mimics – apparently can learn new songs throughout their lives. Either that, or they memorize *all* their songs early in life and only use some of them later. Let's flip a coin to decide which is more amazing.

My own process of learning birdsong is easier to explain: I listen to those *Birding By Ear* tapes for thirty minutes every morning while I exercise, and, very slowly, and with lots of lapses and failures of will, I'm building up my own repertoire of songs. It's a kind of learning I haven't experienced in several decades – repetition, memorization, trying to fix the thing in your mind...then it slips free and you've "forgotten" it..."Damn it, what bird... No, wait! A white-eyed vireo." The capitol of North Dakota is Bismark, and a common yellowthroat goes *witchity, witchity, witchity*. Except that it's frequently more like The capitol of North Dakota is *usually* Bismark, but sometimes it's Bosemark or Bismeek, and occasionally the stress is on the second syllable instead of the first, and Bismark does sound like Misbark but that's another capitol, and Bismark's sister cities are Chip, Ank-ank, and Picky-tucky-tuck.

In a way, it's unfortunate that we have to reduce bird vocalizations to phonetic or figurative renderings we can remember (reduce them even more than our faulty hearing does already, that is) because once I've "learned" that an eastern towhee says *Drink your TE-E-E-E-E-E* or that a field sparrow sounds like a ping pong ball bouncing on a table, I can never again fully appreciate those songs strictly for the beauty of the sounds themselves. It's like explicating a poem: the analysis can never be more than a shadow of the poem itself. Nevertheless, since humans learning birdsong are like college freshmen reading poetry, the verbal crutches of various kinds do come in handy. You thus discover that not only do towhees have a fixation on tea but that yellow warblers have a fixation on sugar (*Sweet, sweet, sweet, little more sweet!*); red-headed woodpeckers are homophobic (*Queer...queer...*); great horned owls are (surprised?) insomniacs (*Who's awake? Me, too.*);

red-eyed vireos are always losing track of each other (*Here I am. Where are you?*); chestnut-sided warblers are always *Pleased, pleased, pleased to MEET'cha*; barred owls are possessed of a certain culinary nosiness (*Who cooks for you? Who cooks for you alllllll?*); olive-sided flycatchers have been known to knock back a few (*Quick! Three beers!*); and warbling vireos are excessively affectionate (*When I SEE you I will SEIZE you and I'll SQUEEZE you till you SHIT!*). That one I didn't learn from my tapes.

Some birds' vocabularies are extremely limited (*Three-eight... Bubble-zee... Conquer-eee... Bee-buzz...*), and others are apparently content just to talk nonsense (*Chiva-chiva... Peet-teet... Skeow!...*). It doesn't help any that ornithologists, for all their scientific precision in their experiments with birds, can't seem to get the hang of words themselves. For example, most warblers don't warble; the American tree sparrow breeds in the treeless Arctic; the northern and Louisiana waterthrushes are not thrushes nor "water" thrushes but warblers; the yellow-breasted chat is a...warbler; the winter wren does take part in the other three seasons; the vesper sparrow sings at all times of the day; neither the Nashville nor the Tennessee warblers has much connection with that state except to pass through it on their way to Canada, where they, along with most of the other fifty-four species of wood-warblers, share breeding grounds with the...Canada warbler; the American redstart does, I guess, "start" to be red, if orange is a start; purple finches are not purple but...red; the blue-headed vireo's head is gray; the ring-necked duck's neck-ring is virtually invisible whereas its bill-ring is easily seen; the common nighthawk is not a hawk, nor is it only active at night; the prairie warbler mostly avoids the Great Plains; the pronthonotary warbler, I feel safe in assuming, is rarely seen in courtrooms; and the tufted titmouse does have a tuft but no "tits," nor does it resemble a mouse.

But learning birdsong is adding new mystery to my sense of "outside," and I wouldn't go back to a duller sense of that dimension even if I could. True, I can't watch a movie anymore or even a TV commercial without trying to identify the birds singing in the background. And my wife grows weary of being quizzed about birds ("Know what that was?") she hasn't even heard. But it's comforting somehow – as I sit on the deck in the evenings, fast approaching half a century, listening intently to the sprinklings of avian music all around – to know that there is a world forever joined to our own, just outside the door, that no one will ever completely understand.

Note

A note to birders, especially "ear" birders: I wrote this essay at the only point in my learning of birdsong that I could have, i.e. when I thought I was better at identifying birds in the field by ear than I was. I tried to write it a year earlier, when I *was* just starting to learn birdsong, but couldn't. Now, several years later, I also would not be able to write it because I've learned so much more.

Pocket Wildernesses, and the Good Dr Pepper Defiled

A "pocket wilderness" – in Tennessee, at least, where I first encountered the term and where I currently reside – is a small area of forested land left "natural" by the timber or paper company that owns both it and the much larger area of land, comprised of clear-cut forests and pine plantations, that surrounds it. It is not a wilderness at all in the true sense, of course, and the quaint "pocket" label is both a contradiction in terms – real wilderness cannot exist in isolated allotments – and an admission on the part of the timber companies, no doubt unintended, of how little they have left us to enjoy. Moreover, virtually all of Tennessee is second and third growth – loggers having taken, by the early part of the twentieth century, every acre of old growth the terrain would allow – so "wilderness" is inapplicable in that sense, too.

Still, if you're a hiker, these remnants are nice to have, and the timber companies clearly want us to think they're nice, and that they, the timber companies, are nice also, for leaving these tiny tracts "wild." They've built trails and established campsites, and in their literature praise themselves (calling themselves "foresters") for having preserved the pocket wildernesses, and speak as if their timber business exists solely for the purpose of supporting their magnanimous deeds. They speak of the "excellent habitat" that "young pine forests" (their tree farms) provide wildlife, meaning by "wildlife" perhaps horseflies and gnats. They speak of clear-cutting as a means of "regenerating the forest" when all it really does, in the twenty to fifty years it takes their single-species pines to become "harvestable," is regenerate timber. They compare their multi-million-dollar industry to backyard gardening, speaking of their "genetically-improved Loblolly pines" as having the same requirements of sunlight and moisture "that familiar garden vegetables such as tomatoes and corn have." "Gardening," of course, requires "both mechanical tilling and/or herbicides," which are used to reduce the "competition" from "unmerchantable" trees and (to polish off dozens of species of flora with a single word) "brush." "Please Excuse Our Mess. New Forest in Progress," implores the placard which stands at the trailhead of one of these pockets, and from which the above quotations have been taken. The "mess," apparently, is the ravaged hillside behind you that doesn't fade from memory as you start up the trail.

Doesn't fade in part because it follows you *up* the trail, only now it's a different category of mess. It's the people-mess at campsites with which hikers all over America, exploring faux-wilderness or real, are all too familiar because they produce it, or at least a prolific class of them does. I'm not going to preach a sermon about the wastefulness of my countrymen – everyone already knows that – but it does strike me as at least peculiar that someone interested enough in checking out the natural world to struggle their way into it up rocky trails and in fickle weather would then defile it by leaving their garbage behind. A recent experience with this little conundrum is what this essay is about, but it's also (oddly enough) about Dr Pepper.

Soft drinks have their deep origins in eighteenth-century European attempts to duplicate the effervescent qualities of natural mineral-spring water, which was thought to have medicinal value, but in this country they began in the pharmaceutical business. Pharmacists were forever tinkering with different combinations of herbs, roots, and fruit juices to produce tonics with supposed curative powers that also tasted good, and in 1885 in Waco, Texas, either Wade B. Morrison or Charles C. Alderton, depending upon which "history" you read, first produced and named this country's oldest soft drink (Coca-Cola appeared the following year), Dr Pepper. Dr. Charles T. Pepper, a Virginia pharmacist for whom Morrison had once worked, lent, involuntarily, only his name. One story has it that Morrison had fallen in love with Pepper's daughter, to the doctor's disapproval – was fired, moved to Waco, threw himself despairingly into tonic-making, and named his beverage (originally, Dr Pepper's Phos-Ferrates) out of addled, lovesick respect for the young lady's father. Another is that Alderton, Morrison's Waco assistant, invented the drink, and named it Dr Pepper as an inside joke between him and his boss. So: homage or irony. Take your pick. I know which one I prefer.

All soft drinks were originally marketed as having health-enhancing properties (Coke could cure everything from "biliousness" to "mental exhaustion," and 7Up was first promoted as a hangover remedy), and Dr Pepper, especially with its prophylactic name, was no exception. An early slogan was "Good For Life," another "Liquid Sunshine," but the most successful was the "10, 2, and 4" theme. In 1927 a Columbia University professor, doing research on "daily human fatigue," had discovered that people's energy levels dropped at mid-morning, mid-afternoon, and late-afternoon, and Dr Pepper decided to capitalize on this finding with the line, "Drink a Bite to Eat at 10, 2, and 4!" This, combined with the usual sex (an early poster shows a long-legged flapper in a bathing suit thrusting high a bottle of the brew and proclaiming, "Come and get it!"), carried Dr Pepper out of Texas and into the rest of the country, into the cities, into the towns – and eventually into a certain pocket wilderness in Tennessee.

○

On a short backpacking excursion recently, a simple over-nighter, my wife and I passed the filthiest campsite I have ever seen. We didn't bother to look closely, didn't want to look closely, just agreed that on our way back the next day we would clean it up. Since the site was only a couple of miles into an eight-mile hike, it would not be that difficult to bag the stuff up (there were cans, soft-drink bottles, other trash, even clothes: that much did register) and lug it out.

Long, steep hike. Magnificent falls at the end. Relatively clean campsite.

On the way up we had passed some sort of church group on their way down, eight or ten people wearing similarly-silkscreened T-shirts, and wondered if good-Samaritanism extended to trashed-out campsites in pocket wildernesses. But, no, apparently not. Though with a party that large, a modest amount of garbage per person would have left the site clean, when we returned, there it was in all its splendor. Now, since we had to, we took stock: empty cans and boxes and wrappers; empty packs of MREs; spent containers of Sterno; those disposable glow-stick things; cigarette butts (filtered); a half-eaten jar of peanut butter; a half-burned, balled-up plastic tarp of some sort; a pair of men's underwear, a pair of socks, even a sweatshirt (all soaked from recent rains)...and seven or eight 20-ounce plastic bottles of Dr Pepper, capped and nearly all filled, but not with the beverage. "Stream water," is what I guess I thought as I began unscrewing caps and emptying bottles, but I don't actually recall thinking much of anything. The liquid did have the not-quite-clear tint of the stream only yards away, one of many in Tennessee permanently poisoned by run-off from early-twentieth-century strip mines. Then, as I was draining perhaps the third container, my wife said, "Wait a minute. What's in those bottles?" – and we looked at each other, and both of us already knew. I took a tentative sniff, and yes, no doubt about it: human urine. Seven or eight 20-ounce plastic Dr Pepper bottles filled with urine.

"I don't know, Michael. That's body fluid," said my wife after we had registered our disgust and I'd resumed the emptying. So I checked my fingers for cuts, found none, and continued. Fifteen minutes later we were headed back down the trail, I with an extra twenty pounds of garbage strapped to my pack, which we disposed of in the trash can at the trailhead.

Forget good Samaritan – I'd just like to know what would cause a person (no, several persons, all with robust bladders) not only to leave behind their trash, even perfectly good clothes, but deliberately to urinate in their empty soft-drink bottles, then cap them off, and leave them for others to find.

"Maybe they didn't know they could pee on the ground," offered my wife, casting me a doubtful glance even as she spoke.

But, no, since females are not endowed with the gift of aim, since the underwear was male, since it's hard to imagine any male not knowing he could pee on the ground, and since pee-on-the-ground decorum had not been logically extended to include other forms of restraint, my good wife's decorous theory was hard to accept.

Unless (could it be?) we weren't dealing here with vermin, with Neanderthals, with worms, but something approaching saints! whose intention was to pack out even their bodily wastes when, alas, one of those thrice-daily energy slumps had hit, the elixir was gone, and they barely made it out with themselves.

Or maybe they'd read the timber company's placard at the start of the trail, and were filled with such radical-environmentalist moral outrage at the corporation's claim that it must rape the land to save it, that they sacked the place as an expression of their purist wrath. Like Edward Abbey in one of his essays tossing Schlitz cans for hundreds of miles out the window of his '62 Dodge as he drives back home to Wolf Hole, because "it's not the beer cans that are ugly; it's the highway."

It would have somehow made more sense if the soft-drink bottles *had* been beer cans, but they weren't; alcohol consumption was nowhere in evidence. I myself had hauled my own four beers up to the falls, but here... just soft-drink-sipping slovenry. And slovenry that, to a certain extent, had to have been planned, given the quantity of urine they'd managed to produce. No, there was purposefulness to this act, a thumb of the nose at both the natural world and the human, an inarticulate, scatter-shot "Fuck you" at things in general. They'd hiked their measly couple of miles to this spot, perhaps gotten bored, decided that "Camping sucks," and devised this clever expression of their imbecile wrath.

And so what are we finally to think? What is the moral of our little story?

Only this: One class of wilderness is certain *always* to survive, a wilderness encircled not by clear-cut forests but bone – that ever-mysterious wilderness of the human mind.

Paul Bunyan Lives!

I hadn't thought about Paul Bunyan in decades.

He was the focus of one of my reading phases as a kid – like my "Allabout Books" phase and my Hardy Boys phase – but, as with those, my enthusiasm flagged as quickly as it had been fired, and I simply forgot him the way you forget lots of transitory interests. Paul and his blue ox Babe, the Round River, that giant pancake griddle that they greased by skating around on it with slabs of bacon strapped to their feet – those stories entertained me until they ceased to entertain me and I haphazardly progressed to the next stage in my reading.

The question and her initial reply were the usual ones after my 8-year-old stepdaughter had tumbled into the car.

"So what did you learn in school today?"

"Nothing. ...Well, we learned about this guy. Old Pa or something."

"Who?"

"Old Pa. He made the Rocky Mountains and dug the Miss...the Missus... that river."

"The Mississippi? You mean Paul Bunyan?"

"Yeah, him."

At home she turned to the two pages in her third-grade social studies book where Paul Bunyan was discussed. There he was in all his towering glory, digging the Mississippi as a more efficient means of transporting his logs, his flung shovelsful of dirt taking shape behind him as the Rocky Mountains. The verdant Mississippi Valley, unaccountably already dotted with log cabins, stretched beneath him, grasslands intact, trees lush and full, and not a stump in sight.

"So you see," concluded the short textbook article, "how the Paul Bunyan stories are not real but just *tall tales*."

Thinking back to our exchange, I wasn't entirely sure Amanda did see. And I wasn't sure, now, that I did either.

Michael O'Rourke

O

Paul Bunyan clearly is a relic of an earlier time even if he did show up in a third-grade social studies text in the year 2002. Why, then, did he show up? Well, because he's also America's most popular folk hero – apparently the longest lasting, and the one about whom the most has been written. I flipped through the rest of Amanda's book and found no mention of Pecos Bill, John Henry, or Old Stormalong – all fictions – nor of the fictions that were created about Mike Fink, Davy Crockett, or John ("Johnny Appleseed") Chapman. Then I typed "Paul Bunyan" as a key word into the Library of Congress's on-line catalog, and this message appeared: "Your search retrieved more records than can be displayed. Only the first 10,000 will be shown."

But he's still a relic (right?) not only because he's a "hero" who cuts down trees but because he does it with such gusto and so wantonly, felling dozens of trees with one swing of his mighty ax, mowing down (with Babe's help) whole sections at a time. He's a clear cutter's clear cutter – ravaging entire landscapes with impunity, then simply leaving the carnage behind to ravage more. How could such a folk hero – Library of Congress holdings or no – be anything but an anachronism? Who in their right mind could take these stories seriously now?

But of course the Paul Bunyan tall tales were never meant to be taken seriously...right? They're just that, *tall tales* – preposterous exaggerations whose primary purpose is to entertain. They're innocuous children's stories, or at least that's what they've become: to whom has it ever occurred to read Paul Bunyan as an adult? An enormous, fictional lumberjack who dwarfs the natural world, who creates its most splendid features, who often does so for the purpose of making use of them in meeting his ever-expanding commercial needs – not to mention who flattens forests – could never have been, nor could ever be, anything but harmless fun.

Right?

O

American Indians have their myths; likewise, Europeans. European-Americans do not. Instead, most of us white folks who call ourselves American have folklore and tall tales (of course the former have folklore, too).

Myth, first of all (and much folklore), springs from sources far too old for a country with only a couple of centuries under its belt. Also, myth – and I'm speaking here in very general terms and as someone considerably lower in status than a rank amateur on the subject – is "religious" in its concerns (gods and goddesses, etc.), and the U. S. of A., our protestant fundamentalist brethren notwithstanding, is basically a secular nation. Folk-tales, like myth-tales, are transmitted orally from generation to generation until someone writes them down, but are not always ancient in origin, are more rooted in the world of ordinary human experience than myths, and are more concerned with matters of social conduct and misconduct than the metaphysical conundrums that myth tries to solve, like —Why are we here?

The tall tale is a kind of American sub-genre of folktale. (It is, in fact, like all literary genres, as old as civilization, but that it found its most favorable growing conditions in nineteenth-century America is not in dispute.) It is a product of the American frontier and our "conquest" of it. That vast area west of the Mississippi (that's where I'm placing the "frontier," but west, of course, is farther east the farther back in time you go), seemingly infinite in size and fraught with all manner of danger, called for folk heros with the vitality and the audacity to take it on, and so characters like Pecos Bill – who was raised by coyotes and could wrestle cyclones to the ground – and Paul Bunyan were born. The tall tale's humor was as broad as the landscape. But it was a short-lived genre because, contrary to Thomas Jefferson's prediction that it would take a hundred generations to settle the western half of the continent that Lewis and Clark had traversed in 1804-1806, by the late nineteenth century (the country's first transcontinental railroad was completed in 1869) the frontier was effectively gone.

Paul Bunyan lasted longer than Pecos Bill, Mike Fink, Davy Crockett *et al* because the logging industry didn't reach its early zenith (and the eastern forests their nadir) until the latter 1800's. As the loggers moved down through Maine and across New England and the Great Lakes States – wreaking havoc as they went – then jumped first to the Southern forests and soon afterward to the West, Paul Bunyan stories went with them and were supposedly swapped, oneupmanship-style, around the campstove at night. I say "supposedly" for a reason. Almost nothing is known for certain about the stories' origins or their life in the lumber camps. A few early "collectors" of the Bunyan tales claim to know – most absurdly James Stevens, who in the Introduction to his 1925 book *Paul Bunyan*, asserts with the utmost confidence that Paul Bunyon was a celebrated warrior on the

French-Canadian side in the Papineau Rebellion of 1837 and later "operated a logging camp" (1), but subsequent scholars have found no evidence to support the claims. (Perhaps Stevens' assertion is itself a "tall tale"? I don't think so. More about Stevens later.)

Maybe there was a real-person prototype for the Paul Bunyan character, maybe not. No one knows. Maybe the tales had their origins in New Brunswick, maybe Maine, maybe the Great Lakes states. No one knows. Such scant records exist of straight-from-the-logger's-mouth Bunyan stories, and so quickly did Paul Bunyan, once he hit print, become the province of professional writers with agendas of their own, that eminent folklorist Richard Dorson has asserted (with a tad more credibility than James Stevens) that Paul Bunyan is not folklore but "fakelore." He's largely a literary concoction, says Dorson, a manufactured symbol of the "American Spirit," that much-lauded mixture of energy and ingenuity (and avarice and exploitation?) that enabled us to subdue an entire continent.

Well, I'm not so sure how "fake" that sounds to me in other ways. And since folklore isn't my line, that *Only the first 10,000 will be shown* computer message still perplexes.

O

Paul Bunyan first appeared in print in a story by one James MacGillivray entitled "The Round River Drive" that was published by the *Detroit News-Tribune* in 1910. "What!" begins the story. "You never heard of the Round River drive? Don't suppose you ever read about Paul Bunyan neither?" (Felton 335). And that's the first of only a handful of times that Bunyan is even mentioned. He isn't a character in the story, just the named boss of the logging operation. The story itself consists of a series of anecdotes that appear over and over again in subsequent writers' renderings. Other elements that reappear, though in time less blatantly: the trees-are-there-to-be-cut-down timber ethic, and the reference to black kitchen-hands as "coons."

The 10,000-plus flood began as a trickle. Four years later "The Round River Drive," this time by Douglas Malloch, appeared as ear-grating verse in the trade journal *American Lumberman*. Same anecdotes, same name-only Paul Bunyan, but a new moniker for the blacks: this time they're "niggers" as well as "coons" (Felton 341-350).

Lame story in a newspaper, bad verse in a trade journal, four years apart: not a very promising inaugural for the most famous American folk hero of all.

Okay, I know we're talking tall tales here, and I also know that the teller of the tale always insists upon its truth, but this next part is *not* a tall tale – and I insist upon its truth.

Paul Bunyan's very first reasonably wide audience was reached not via a book or mainstream magazine (children's stories, perhaps? maybe a piece in *Atlantic Monthly?*) but an advertising pamphlet for...a lumber company. To wit: the Red River Lumber Company of Minnesota. The pamphlet author's name? (Now remember, I wouldn't lie to you.) Laughead. To wit: W. B. Laughead, an ex-logger himself. (Yes, maybe it's pronounced "Loff-ed," but I refuse to withdraw my joke.) The pamphlet was postcard-sized (first edition, 1914, 32 pages in length) and alternated advertising copy with short Bunyan stories. But Laughead hadn't properly analyzed his audience of wholesalers and other middlemen, who didn't know a peavey from a petunia, so in 1916 and again in 1922 he revised his pamphlet, substituting standard and even finance-and-marketing English for the lumberjack lingo, and its popularity zoomed. Between 1922 and 1944, the year of its Thirtieth Anniversary Edition, in excess of 100,000 copies were distributed. Paul Bunyan wasn't an American folk hero yet, but he sure as hell was American.

○

There isn't a lot of *oohing* and *ahhing* about the "Great American Forest" in the written records that the first European-Americans left behind. Magnificent pristine wilderness? Forget it. The forests were, to them, mostly a barrier and a threat – a barrier to the development of agriculture and to further expansion, and a threat comprised of, first and foremost, the "Vast Unknown," and second, increasingly hostile (the more they were given the shaft) "savages." The ocean of trees these people encountered had no precedent in Europe – or rather, its precedent was centuries gone. They couldn't live off the forest like the Indians had been doing since paleolithic times because they didn't possess the knowledge that only thousands of years of experience of living off the forest could yield. Farming is all they knew: they had to farm. And so for the better part of two centuries, millions of acres of trees were simply cut and burned, wasted, for the purpose of clearing the land for crops. Some obviously were used in construction – and some of the biggest white pines went for ship masts – but this was prior to the great westward expansion, and untold multitudes of trees during this period, along with the habitats they made possible for all manner of creatures, were just nullified.

Brief aside: How did those Indians live off the forest? Interestingly enough, also by burning trees, but constructively. In his highly informative and exhaustively researched (the bibliography runs to 75 pages) book entitled *America's Ancient Forests*, Thomas M. Bonnicksen, himself of Osage descent, explains that American Indians couldn't live off the forest as it was either. Too dense. Too many places for animals to hide. Too hard to hunt. So, wherever they hunted and lived, they burned, but in a way that actually enhanced the forest and increased the wildlife instead of the reverse. Each fall they set ground fires in the region to which they planned to return in the spring. The outcome was that large trees were unharmed (and grew larger, producing, in the case of the nut-bearing trees, more nuts for people and animals alike) but saplings and brush were burned off and were then replaced the following spring, with nutrient-rich grasses and shrubs that attracted game that were now easier to hunt in the more open forest. Early explorers and settlers did *ooh* and *ahh* a bit over these huge park-like woodlands. Botanist and writer William Bartram, circa 1773 (his book *Travels* will describe for you what is now gone forever in the Southeast): "We rose gradually a sloping bank...and immediately entered this sublime forest. The ground is perfectly a level green plain, thinly planted by nature with the most stately forest trees, such as the gigantic black oak,...whose mighty trunks, seemingly of an equal height, appeared like superb columns" (Bonnicksen 231). Colonist Andrew White describing the Potomac River forests in 1633: "On each bank of solid earth rise beautiful groves of trees, not choked up with an undergrowth of brambles and bushes, but as if laid out by hand, in a manner so open that you might drive a four-horse chariot in the midst of the trees" (Bonnicksen 265).

Fire was also used to produce clearings in which Indians grew their own crops, or to create and maintain meadows to which animals were naturally attracted and thus more easily hunted, or to drive animals into or away from areas where the Indians did or did not want them to be. One result of these open forests was that bison roamed as far east as Pennsylvania and New York. Another, and intended, result was that dangerous wildfires were prevented, a lesson us pale-faces have learned far too late, and we pay the price for our ignorance every summer now in the West.

Look. What's the big deal about cutting and burning all those zillions of trees? The Great American Forest is inexhaustible (they believe). It's infinite (they believe). You could cut, burn, bulldoze, pave, "multiple use" it forever and never come to the end of it.

Right?

○

Daniel Hoffman wrote the only book-length study of the Paul Bunyan tall tales that exists, and it is to his book, *Paul Bunyan: Last of the Frontier Demigods*, that I am indebted for most of the publication history I'm giving you. Hoffman laments the fact that "Ol' Paul" never developed into a *gen-u-ine* national epic hero with an epic literature to match, but partly what I'm trying to do here is to show that, unfortunately, in some ways, he did... and, well, I guess we can forgive Hoffman his lament since his book was published in 1952. However, Aldo Leopold's book was published in 1949 – but, all right, he was ahead of his time. Just like George Perkins Marsh (*Man and Nature*, 1864) was ahead of his time, and John Burroughs and John Muir and Thoreau and Edward Abbey – all, all ahead of their times.

The first actual Paul Bunyan book (entitled, aptly enough, *Paul Bunyan*) was written by Esther Shephard and published in 1924. Hoffman doesn't like it (as, justifiably, he doesn't like most of the books he discusses; that's part of his lament). He calls it a "careless document," and adds the adjectives "jumbled," "random," "discursive," "undramatic," "disorganized," "meandering," "silly," "dull," "long-winded," "unskilled," and "flat" (87-94).

Hmm. That's a pretty damning assessment by a soon-to-become pretty heavy-duty literary scholar (of Poe and others), but I think the book is pretty okay – taking into consideration, of course, that almost all the Paul Bunyan "literature" is junk. Here's how the book begins: "If what they say is true Paul Bunyan was born down in Maine. And he must of been a pretty husky baby too, just like you'd expect him to be, from knowin' him afterwards" (1).

Well, what's wrong with that? I mean, besides the fact that no adult would want to read an entire book about Paul Bunyan – and both this and the next two books I intend to drag you through were aimed at an adult audience. Shephard creates a kind of passable vernacular for her narrator – who knows if it's "accurate" – and though Hoffman sees "meandering," etc. as a fault, that quality strikes me as completely intentional on Shephard's part. The stories do meander, each one winding in and out of the others

– rather skillfully associatively linked, if you ask me – and that's the way the "original" tales were supposedly (maybe) told around that campstove. I think Hoffman just got sick of reading Paul Bunyan books – and who can blame him?

In Shephard, and in every subsequent Bunyan book, Bunyan *is* a principle player. He does all the stuff you vaguely remember: "logs off" North Dakota; makes it through the "Winter of the Blue Snow"; finally figures out that that river they've been endlessly running logs down, getting nowhere, is round (Paul isn't always real bright); kills boatloads of "wild animals" ("The way he got wolves was, he just scared 'em to death hollerin' at 'em") (109) and shiploads of trees; imports giant bumblebees to eat the giant mosquitoes that have been plaguing his men, only to find that the two species mate and produce offspring with stingers at both ends (mosquitoes, by the way, were the real "wild animals" in a logger's life – the others cleared out in advance of the ruin); inadvertently digs the Grand Canyon when, hot and tired, he drags his peavey across the desert; digs the Mississippi and St. Lawrence rivers; digs the Columbia River; digs Puget Sound; creates the Rockies and the Alleghenies; creates Great Salk Lake "to have salt on hand for Babe" (187)...etc.

Oh yes, and "niggers" make their appearance in Shephard's book:

Instead of twenty men with slabs of bacon on their feet skatin' around greasin' the griddle, Paul had eighty now – most of 'em niggers, because bein' from Africa they could stand the heat better. Though a few of 'em wasn't swift enough like they should be. The minute the whistle blowed it was up to them flunkies to get out of the way, or, the way that batter poured in – well, sometimes we just naturally had a raisin in the hotcake, that was all. (124)

Since Shephard's a woman, and it's 1924, and she's only been able to vote (astounding!) for the last four years, you'd think...but, no, I guess not.

A few glimmers of nascent "environmental awareness" do creep into the book. After Bunyan logs off North Dakota and pounds the stumps into the ground so that the "socialist Swedes" can settle there...

...he was leavin' the country, sure, as good, or a good deal better than he found it, and that's more than can be said for a good deal of loggin' that's done. It's a rotten shame the way they leave some of it, as if a cyclone had struck it, and never a stick would grow there no more. Just rocks and stumps and splinters, and young trees all tore up." (144)

But most of the time it's more like this:

But if Paul was goin' to do any loggin' he'd have to get some land first because he didn't have no land claims out here [the West], and he'd have to come by it some way, and the way he done that was by homesteadin', and by scrippin' [phony entitlements]. He could get a lot of land by scrippin'. Because he could go ahead and scrip some land and then when he'd get all the timber cleared off he could explain that he'd made a mistake and scripped the wrong land and go ahead and scrip some more. That way he could keep right on goin'. And for the homesteadin', he didn't do that himself, of course – he'd get other men to do it for him. He'd get fellers who didn't care much whether they told the truth or not to swear that they was gettin' timber claims for themselves, as homesteaders, and then he'd pay 'em fifty dollars for their deed, and get the land that way. Sometimes – like some of the other timber men did, too – he could get dead men to take up homesteads for him and then he didn't have to pay the fifty dollars. (147)

Is that encomium or opprobrium? Well, whatever it is, she's got her facts straight: fraud in the logging industry was just as rampant as the logging.

The best thing about the book is not the stories (which seem innocent enough if you ignore parts like those I've quoted, and if you don't begin to reflect upon what it *means* that Paul, for example, creates all that geography; he is, after all, a product of our culture whether the tales are authentic folklore or not) but painter Rockwell Kent's illustrations. Kent's Paul Bunyan has a positively fiendish look about him: he relishes flattening those forests. And the landscape over which he and Babe tower is in several drawings not a pretty sight to see.

Just light entertainment, these tall tales? Perhaps. But Kent seems to have detected in them something darker.

○

They came to the end of the Great Lakes Forest – in the U.S., that's Michigan, Wisconsin, and Minnesota – in fifty years. Originally, 85% of those three states was forested. Michigan and Wisconsin were almost completely forested. They leveled them. Now, after extensive re-planting during the New Deal thirties, the figure is 43%, and virtually the only old growth left is in Michigan's Porcupine Mountains Wilderness State Park on the shores of Lake Superior.

By the mid-nineteenth century, and especially following the Civil War, rapidly increasing immigration and baby-making – accompanied by the migration of Americans ever-westward and the consequent growth of cities like Chicago, Detroit, and St. Louis – had so depleted the Northeastern forests (New York and Pennsylvania got the worst of it) that the Timber Barons began to look longingly at the Northwest, which at that time was the three above-named states.

Of course, first they had to get the forested lands away from the Indians, who held legal (ha-ha) "right to occupy" title, but that was easy: just, you know, sign some more "treaties."

So, okay, the Eastern forests weren't inexhaustible. The Great Lakes forests were: they were sure of it. Like...well, for example, the passenger pigeon, most populous bird on the planet (not North America, the planet) when the first Europeans arrived – current estimates, 3-5 billion. No way we're ever going to run out of *those* little feathered critters. But by the late nineteenth century, it had been so massively hunted for food and "sport" (those "clay pigeons" used for target practice? – well, originally they weren't clay) and its habitat so massively destroyed that its extinction was assured. The last known wild one was shot by an Ohio farm boy, who didn't know any better, in 1900, and the last one of all (Martha, they had named her) died in the Cincinnati Zoo in 1914.

But back to our story. Heck, you can see a passenger pigeon (and a Carolina parakeet, and an ivory-billed woodpecker, and a heath hen, and a Labrador duck, and a great auk, and...) anytime you want. Just go to your nearest big-city natural history museum.

The idea was that you cut the trees, sell them to your burgeoning markets in the cities, then sell the land for farmland. This worked pretty well in the southern half of the three states under discussion, not nearly as well in the northern. The soil was thin, with bedrock not far below – fine for trees, not fine for crops. (Not much was known about soils at the time.) Lots of people tried to realize their American Dream on those soils, lots of people failed. It was a mess.

It was a mess in many other ways as well...

Wait a minute. When you mow down forests, does that affect the climate? Does the weather get hotter and drier? And does that raise the likelihood of wildfires?

Seems that all those things happen, and more.

Logging practices were incredibly wasteful and destructive. Even in a book I found, published in 1934, entitled *Logging: The Principles and Methods of Harvesting Timber in the United States and Canada* by Nelson C. Brown, Professor of "Forest Utilization" at New York State College of Forestry in Syracuse – not a book in which you'd expect to find an over-abundance of environmental sensitivity – the phrases "great wastage" and "enormous wastage" appear several times in the brief history of logging Nelson provides. Enormous indeed. First of all, while the biggest trees lasted (and the giant white pines were what they went after first), they didn't even use the whole tree. They'd lop off the top and all the branches, and simply leave them there with the stumps, the cut and uncut brush (this was all "slash"), and the smaller and "unmerchantable" trees and saplings. Then, almost inevitably, fires would follow. Sometimes these fires were deliberately set (for "stump farm"-making purposes), sometimes not, but all too often they were quickly out of control. Again, millions of acres burning, but this time much hotter fires because of the slash and the climate-altering effects of such colossal (and historically unprecedented) forest-destruction in one geographical region. (We wrote the book now being avidly read in the world's rainforests.) Forests that otherwise would have been able, in time – much time – to regenerate themselves were now reduced to ash and virtually sterilized soil. What follows the fires? Flooding, erosion, stream silting, fish-kill, fish-species extinction, and a generally not-nice-to-look-at landscape.

The Peshtigo fire in Wisconsin in 1871 is the one my sources kept bringing up, probably because it killed over 1100 people. It's even in the *Encyclopedia Britannica*. It incinerated 1,200,000 acres, including the town of Peshtigo itself. But there were many, many others. Here's a quote from Robert F. Fries' 1951 book *Empire in Pine: The Story of Lumbering in Wisconsin, 1830-1900*, another book that doesn't exactly go overboard (you can deduce his bias from the title) in talking about environmental destruction:

> In 1885 nearly all of an eighty-mile strip in the Wisconsin River valley was swept by fire. In 1905 fires broke out in nearly every one of the thirty-two counties of northern Wisconsin, a total of 1,435 in all, which burned over more than a million acres and sent up a pall of smoke that sometimes impeded navigation on Lake Michigan as far south as Chicago. (246)

It was the fires that finally began to awaken the public to the fact that maybe something was wrong here.

But while we're on the subject of burning, how about this little tidbit? The modern iron industry started (and then boomed for fifty years) in

Michigan's Upper Peninsula. But – guess what? – in the beginning, they didn't use coal for fuel.

As Fries' title makes clear, pine, preferably white pine, is what the early lumbermen most wanted because it was easy to work with and it floated high in the water (for the spring drives). Heavier woods sank. So the "heavier" woods were left behind, to see if they could survive the fires.

Then the railroads, which gradually supplanted river transportation of logs and also, along with other technological advances, made those "heavier" woods transportable. Transportable where? Why, to the ironworks, of course, to be converted into charcoal for the smelting of iron. Oak! Hickory! Maple! Beech! Elm! Walnut! Yellow poplar!

Charcoal.

O

I'm being awfully mean here. I'll try to be nicer about our next Paul Bunyan author, James Stevens.

Nope. Can't.

(Hoffman, our scholar, isn't nice about him, so that gives me license.)

Stevens' book, also entitled *Paul Bunyan*, was published right on the heels of Esther Shephard's 1924 book, in 1925. Both caused something of a stir in literary and ethnographic circles because here was Paul Bunyan "folklore" being given book-length treatment, and wide circulation, for the first time.

Hoffman thinks Stevens' book stinks (he's right), albeit for different reasons than the ones suggested by that string of adjectives he flings at Shephard's book. But he also thinks that Stevens' *Paul Bunyan* – despite the fact that most of the "tales" he tells aren't funny at all, aren't in the tall tale tradition, and don't get picked up by subsequent writers – is responsible for the American "Superhero" image that we now take for granted in the Bunyan character.

This I just did not get, having dozed my way through Stevens' awful book only once. So I read the damn thing a second time (and you'd better thank me because now you don't have to read it even once), and yes, unfortunately – but with implications arising from Stevens' book that Hoffman probably didn't have in mind – again, I think he's right.

Stevens, you remember, is the guy who, in the Introduction to his book, claims to know that the Bunyan tales derive from the historical figure (whom no historian has found) Paul Bunyon, who participated in that rebellion up in Quebec and later turned to logging. He also states forthrightly that each lumber camp had a "camp bard" who, with colleagues in rapt attendance around the campstove each night, "could take one of the key stories and elaborate on it for hours, building a complete narrative, picturing awe-inspiring characters, inventing dialogue of astonishing eloquence" (6). (This after both he and his buddies had worked – literally – from dawn to dusk at one of the most grueling and dangerous jobs this side of Egyptian pyramid construction.)

Let's sample some other quotes from his Introduction:

> The art of the plain American, which in the last century brought forth tales and songs as native to the soil as the grass of the prairies [long perished], is at last perishing *under the feet of the herd arts of a perfected democratic culture.* [emphasis, I happily acknowledge, mine] (6)

> This art is perishing simply because Universal Education, *and other blights, curses and evil inventions of democracy* are destroying all the old simplicity, imaginativeness and self-amusement of plain American life. [yes, me] (7)

> [American loggers] made their Paul Bunyan an inventor and orator, and an industrialist whose labors surpassed those of Hercules. [no, sorry, that's your little plan, James] (4)

And:

> [The Bunyan "legend"] is true American legend now, for Paul Bunyan, as he stands today, is absolutely American from head to foot. [time perhaps to sigh?] (7)

Hoffman, to his credit (in McCarthyist 1952), calls this tripe "Superpatriotism." I, not having to wear the mantle of an objective literary critic, call it, in addition to tripe, fascism.

In the Introduction to his 1932 follow-up book *The Saginaw Paul Bunyan* (yes, I slogged my way through that one also), Stevens, who, like advertising-pamphlet-writer Laughead, had also worked as a logger – and then, similar to Laughead, became a PR man for the West Coast Lumberman's Association – (but remember: Paul Bunyan is not propaganda, but folklore...repeat after me: folklore), tells us...

By the time the down on my chest had grown into a harsh and tawny stubble I myself was fledging into a camp bard. In the summer nights by the smudge fire and in winter nights by the bunkhouse heater I revised the tales of older bards, giving them whatever form the inspiration of the moment revealed. (14)

So let's see just how good a storyteller this Stevens is.

First of all, Stevens' Paul Bunyan is not a string of anecdotal stories that purport, "meanderingly" or not, to imitate the manner in which the original anecdotes were possibly told; it is (dare I grace it with the word?) a "novel."

First sentence of this "novel":

"Paul Bunyan was the one historian of the useful and the beautiful; other writers of history tell only of terrible and dramatic events." (11)

Huh?

Want to go back and compare Esther Shephard's first two sentences with that one and decide which writer gets the privilege of your reading maybe another sentence?

By page five we learn that our protagonist (soon to become not only "historian" and, of course, "mighty logger," but "inventor," "leader-hero," and "master orator") is a "student" living in a cave in Canada and dining exclusively on raw moose meat.

What? Doesn't make sense? Isn't funny? Isn't anything? Well, hey, maybe this is, like, proto-post-modernist, deconstructionist, semiotic metafiction or something. Maybe our man Stevens is a genius.

So, anyway, since Bunyan is this really smart renaissance-type dude, "he was not long in learning all the history worth knowing" (wonder how many historians reach that conclusion), and "vague ambitions began to stir in his soul." Trouble is, these ambitions are so *confoundedly* vague that, even though he "dream[s] about them" we're never given any clue as to their substance (16).

Then it happens (nine agonizing pages later).

In a dream he sees the "great blazing letters...REAL AMERICA." He wakes up, all confused-like, falls asleep, dreams again, and "in this second dream he saw no words, but a forest. A flame like a scythe blade sheared through the trees and they fell. Then Paul Bunyan saw in his dream a forest of stumps, and trees were fallen among them." (25)

(I'm not making this up, folks. Go read it for yourself.)

Even though Paul's "student's life was finally over; there was nothing more for him to learn," it takes him "many days," "many nights," "weeks," a trek to "Real America" with his new-found ox Babe, *and four more pages*, to figure out what the dream means. Here it is:

> Real America was covered with forests. A forest was composed of trees [that's right, Paul]. A felled and trimmed tree was a log [yes...]. Paul Bunyan threw aside his pine tree beard brush and jumped to his feet with a great shout.
>
> "What greater work could be done in Real America than to make logs from trees?" he cried. "Logging! I shall invent this industry and make it the greatest one of all time! I shall become a figure as admired in history as any of the great ones I have read about." (29)

Don't quite know how you "invent logging" when there's already a name for "logging," but let's just not get into that one.

Filled with "an indomitable conquering spirit" (you know, that "Real American" spirit), with "Freedom and Inspiration and Uplift," Bunyan "delivered his first oration"...to Babe. It's been lost to history (darn!) but, Stevens tells us, dealt primarily with how to load Babe up with logs, i.e. with the logs on one side and rocks on the other for ballast. "It was months after this that he made his first improvement, the using of a second bundle of logs, instead of rocks, for ballast." (29)

No, come on. This is satire, right? What else could it possibly be? Who could write this kind of thing with a straight face?

Well, that's part of what had me scratching my head (in between spells of nodding off) all the way through this pathetic waste of...trees. And Stevens does make some lame attempts at satire later on in his book, aiming awkwardly at what every numbskull American loves to hate – intellectuals and poetry. And maybe, in his mind, there *is* some sort of satirical something going on in the passages I've quoted. *But* (number one) I'm just going to have to side with Hoffman, and a couple of other critics he quotes, and conclude that, when it comes to writing fiction, Stevens doesn't know his ass from a hole in the ground – or, as Carl Van Doren more politely put it, "seems never to have quite made up his mind exactly what he wanted to do" (Hoffman 111). *And* (number two) whatever scatter-shot target Stevens' "satire" is intended to hit, you can be sure it isn't the noble profession of offing forests.

So Bunyan, this "kingly figure," this "leader-hero," sets himself up with a crew of "little loggers," who then proceed to "worship" him and hang on his every "master orator" word like puppy dogs. (He's this Monopolist-Capitalist-Industrialist Timber Baron, see. Wouldn't you worship him, too?) He's constantly giving speeches (though, curiously, we're never provided with the full text of one, just occasional pearls of wisdom like "The test of great leadership is originality" and "Meals make the man") (43, 85); constantly struggling mightily to give birth to an idea the size of a flea; and never giving a moment's thought to the implications of his "work," so much so that the "logging off" of this or that region is mentioned almost as an afterthought.

Astonishingly, there are no references to "coons" or "niggers" in the book, but Stevens more than makes up for this failing with a chapter that is preposterously misogynistic ("Women seemed to lack inventiveness especially, and this was man's greatest quality"; beyond knowing how to cook and sew, "women had apparently done nothing") (225) and with a steady stream of contemptuous remarks about the workers ("Their business was not to think, but to fell trees...as thinkers they were no better than prattling children") (195).

Was the book a popular success? Of course! It sold over 75,000 copies.

I'm sure John D. Rockefeller would have liked it. Hitler also.

O

What about those workers? What was their work like?

Well, if you're the camp cook and his "cookee" (assistant), you're up by 3:30 AM. If you're a logger (actually, they were called lumberjacks in the East, loggers in the West), you get to sleep in till 4:30. You eat your plain but stick-to-the-ribs breakfast (beans, pork, bread, molasses, and tea were the monotonous staples), put on plenty of warm clothing, and head out. Why the warm clothing? Because until the last two or three decades of the nineteenth century, you cut the trees in the winter. Why the winter? Because until the railroads made their way into the Northwoods, the only way to transport the logs to the river, which was the only way to get them to the mills in the spring, was with a sled pulled by oxen – and later by horses, when a technique was developed for making ice-roads. If you're a logger, you're either a chopper, a sawyer, a skidder, a swamper, or a teamster. (There was also the clerk, who kept the records; the scaler, who measured the logs; and in the bigger camps, the blacksmith, the carpenter, and the saw-filer.) Choppers, of course, chopped down the trees (originally just with axes, then later with a two-man saw, while pounding wedges into the cut to keep the saw from binding up); sawyers sawed the cut trees into logs for the mill; skidders dragged the logs (with the help of oxen) to the skidway, which led to the road; swampers maintained the roads and skidways and cleared away brush, tree limbs, etc.; and teamsters drove and cared for the teams of oxen and/or horses.

(None of this information, by the way, can be gleaned from Stevens' book. A whole "novel" about logging – the "greatest industry" – written by an ex-logger, and you learn nothing about logging.)

As I've already indicated, early logging was not a walk in the park. A vertical crack could develop in the trunk of the tree while they were cutting it down, and if the problem wasn't corrected immediately, the whole thing could come straight down on the loggers below. (Remember, these are often enormous trees they're felling. In New England, 200-foot-tall white pines – the ship-mast pines – had been common. In the Great Lakes states, they were somewhat "smaller.") Or the intended direction of the tree's fall could suddenly be altered by standing trees, creating obvious additional dangers. Once the logs were stacked on the sleds with a block and tackle – huge piles of logs chained together – they were transported to the frozen river (very carefully, especially on downgrades, which had to be covered with sand or hay by a "road monkey" to prevent runaway sleds), where they were piled again on the riverbank to await the spring thaw. A man called a top-decker had to stand on top of the forming pile to help direct the placement of each log. Errant logs were the cause of many a top-decker's being crushed to death.

In the spring, there were more opportunities for being crushed to death. If you didn't go home to the stump-farm you might have bought to plant crops on land that couldn't sustain them, you might stay for the spring drive (perhaps because you'd blown all your winter's wages on drinking and whoring in the nearest town; these guys, no doubt about it, were a rough and tumble bunch). The spring drives were probably the most physically-taxing and life-threatening part of logging at that time. If you weren't walking for miles each day along the shores of the river, freeing snagged logs, you were riding the logs themselves, in a snowmelt-swollen stream, trying to prevent jams, and maybe slipping and falling and being crushed to a bloodless pulp, or drowning under a mass of logs through which there was no possibility of surfacing.

Then there were the log jams.

In the spring, all the logging operations along one river would be sending all their logs down the same river at the same time. The jams that resulted – from a shallow stretch, or rocks, or a narrowing of the riverbed – could stretch for miles, reach twenty to thirty feet high, and comprise tens of millions of board feet in logs. (A board foot is the amount of wood in a board one foot square and one inch thick.) Teams of horses along each river bank pulling logs out of the water on each side had to be used to break the biggest jams. Also dynamite at times, though that was expensive. But for the "smaller" jams, it was men with their peaveys – long poles with both a pike and a hook on the end, named for their blacksmith inventor – out on the logs themselves, and you'd better hope you can make it back to shore after you've freed the last (the "key") log before the whole mass of them comes thundering down on top of you.

How much did these guys make putting in twelve-hour days at this kind of work? (Toward the end of Stevens' book, one of the "evil inventions" that Stevens' Bunyan vituperates against is the ten-hour day.) Well, the woodsmen, $15 to $25 a month, and board; skilled workers, $30 to $50 a month, and board; the log-drivers, $2 to $3 a day (perhaps because "days" was all some of them lived), and meals.

Not bad for just "seasonal" work, wouldn't you say?

○

Must we subject ourselves to another Stevens book? Yes, we must. But I'll try to keep it brief.

In 1932 Stevens wrote a second – and, thank God, last – Paul Bunyan "novel," *The Saginaw Paul Bunyan* (that's the Saginaw River Valley in Michigan, a huge area that was wiped...well, I guess you wouldn't say "clean," would you?). As far as the writing itself is concerned, this book is maybe a little better than the first one, which isn't saying much because it's just as mind-numbingly boring, but at least you can follow it. Bunyan is still the Industrialist Leader-Hero, still utterly contemptuous of his men (they "had been trying to learn to think...a perilous occupation for his jacks") (67), but his thematic focus, this time, is crystal-clear: it's "Paul Bunyan Does Battle With Nature." In fact, words like "war," "battle," "invasion," and "conquest" (but especially "war") occur repeatedly in the book. He battles two rebellious rivers, two species of recalcitrant trees, various wild animals, even "the weather" – and (need I say it?) always wins.

But of course it's all in good fun, and so we find ourselves agreeing with Stevens completely when he tells us in the Introduction to *this* book that the reason Paul Bunyan has lasted as a folk hero ("a bearded and mackinawed Hercules who moves mountains, tames rivers, subdues hurricanes, slays fearsome beasts, and, above all, rules men with incomparable humanity") while all those other folk heroes have receded into the "wastes of forgotten time" is because of the "kindness in his heart" while those others "have achieved remembrance only as *symbols of the monstrous forces that may be embodied in mankind*" (11).

Sorry, I just couldn't resist the emphasis.

○

Stevens' Paul Bunyan doesn't like the "evil" ten-hour day because the Timber Barons of fact didn't like it. Money-driven oppression – of the natural world, of minorities, of workers – is popular amongst reactionaries.

In the East, the labor movement had been growing since around 1830, but several decades passed before it began to take hold in the lumbering industry. The earlier-referenced Fries (*Empire in Pine*), who is much better at recognizing injustice against humans than against ecosystems, reasons that the logger's "frontier psychology of optimism and a sense of unlimited opportunity" (211) was the culprit, that way of thinking having long since passed from the minds of his big-city factory-slave compatriots back East. Individualism was still in, but solidarity was slow in coming – and hard to achieve logistically, in any case, in this migratory industry.

But the ten-hour day (and higher wages, and better working conditions, and the common "We'll pay you after the logs are milled and sold" practice, not to mention the infamous price-gouging, credit-enslaving company store) kept gnawing at loggers' and millworkers' minds, and strikes, and their attendant violence on both sides, broke out.

Get this. Ever heard of spiking trees? Well, it isn't new. Fries: "One of the most effective devices of the lumber saboteur was to drive a heavy spike into a saw log, which could not then be run into the saw without endangering the lives of the sawyers." (212)

It was all eventually resolved, sort of...

But have you ever noticed how nothing fair ever seems to get resolved without conflict?

O

After Stevens, all subsequent Paul Bunyan "literature" has been for children. As it should be? Well, we'll see.

Paul Bunyan and His Great Blue Ox, "retold" by Wallace Wadsworth and published in 1926, a year after Stevens' first book, kicked off the genre. One thing I like about it is the story Wadsworth "retells" about the black "cook-boys" who grease the giant griddle by skating around on it with sides of bacon strapped to their feet. "Paul had to have negroes for this task, as white men could not stand the heat," he explains to the kids. These "darkey cook-boys" would sometimes get caught in the flood of batter and end up as those "raisin[s] in the cake." But this "usually didn't happen more than two or three times a month" (84-86).

But, all right, since this is 1926, what I like even better is the 1964 edition that my wife picked up for me at the local Goodwill store. On the book jacket are highlighted these words: "This book is listed by the H. W. Wilson Catalog for Junior High Schools as a book of high quality 'vouched for by a representative group of librarians and specialists in children's literature.'"

I suppose emphasis is needed *somewhere*, but I just can't figure out which words to italicize. Maybe it's emphasis enough to recall that something else was published in 1964: the Civil Rights Act.

I like lots of other things about the book, too.

Shall we begin at the beginning?

First four words: "In the lumber woods..." (9)

As a boy, Paul likes to leave his mark, as we humans are wont to do, by stamping his initials, spelled out with hobnails on the soles of his shoes "into everything he came to. It was not very long before all the trees, rocks and everything else for miles around bore the evidence of his new sport so that soon it became hard for him to find a place where he could stamp 'P.B.' without having the new letters become lost among the thousands of earlier sets of his initials" (30).

Later on there's this persistent problem with "wild animals" mainly because, in for example one case, the "Agropelter" (all in fun, all in fun), they have "a special hatred for all mankind." So, of course, Paul must bring a stop to *that*. These pesky varmints are rendered "extinct" because they are "very dangerous to man." Bunyan must "get rid" of them. The way this is done in the case of the "Gumberoos," interestingly enough, is with "the increasing prevalence of [those aforementioned] fires." With the Agropelters, who "hide away in the hollows of dead trees" (maybe like the ivory-billed woodpecker, now likely departed for lack of similar habitat?), Paul makes sure that "not a hollow tree [was] found standing" (40-54).

Having driven all the "dangerous animals" out of that area, our hero's next challenge is the "Hugags," who, in order to sleep, have to lean against trees or something, I forget, but anyway, "After the full crew got to working... it was not very long before the poor Hugags could no longer find places to lean and as a result they soon began perishing for lack of sleep. Nearly all of them died during the winter that Paul had his big camp on the Red River, and it is only very rarely that a stray one has been seen since that time" (78).

That just leaves the "Splinter Cats." "These great animals used to be common in the big woods until Paul Bunyan grew irritated over the amount of good timber they destroyed [looking for bees to eat] and began to exterminate them." Paul's dog Elmer gets so good at hunting the Splinter Cats "that it was not very long that they were about done away with, and finally Paul killed the last one after his dog had dragged it into camp still alive" (145-147).

(I'm tempted to draw an analogy here between the Splinter Cats and our Western cattle- ranchers' persecution of mountain lions, coyotes, and wolves...but no, that would be taking things way too far, wouldn't it?)

But let's not forget about the trees.

In addition to the "tall tale" element ("he pushed his way through the thick timber, bending aside the trees in his road as if they were stalks of grass") (37), it's curious how blandly matter-of-fact is Wadsworth about both flora and fauna destruction:

"Most people today have never heard of [the Gumberoos and Agropelters], having forgotten that long years ago, before most of the forests were cut down..." (41)

"Most of these animals are now extinct because the lumbermen have destroyed their hiding places..." (41)

"Nothing was left of the great forests that had stood on these vast stretches of fertile land excepting the stumps..." (107)

"From this central location [the Big Onion River] he worked all the Lake States, logging off most of the white pine forests of Minnesota, Wisconsin and Michigan..." (125)

"After his Great Drive, Paul Bunyan's work in the Lake States was done, for this drive had included nearly the last of the good timber to be found in all that section of the country. Only small patches were left here and there..." (148)

And finally:

"Men say that [Bunyan] can never die until the last tree is cut down..." (186)

One wonders if those men are right.

O

(I think I can summarize fairly quickly most of the rest of the early children's Paul Bunyan books. Mind if I did that? No?)

My first-edition, Internet-obtained copy of Frank Shay's 1930 book *Here's Audacity!* shows, on its cover, a stern Paul Bunyan, ax over his shoulder, marching resolutely forward into...the "American Future," I suppose. You open it up (this book is a compilation of stories about a variety of folk heroes, Bunyan receiving by far the longest chapter), and the inside cover and facing page reveal more stern-faced heroes, all bent on conquering adversity and other tenacious nouns.

The book itself, however, is the first in the Bunyan canon that actually gave me a few laughs.

Yes, we get the same old "colored boy"/"nigger"/raisin-in-the-batter joke. And Paul's wife is "ugly and she had a wooden leg" [and is] "just as dumb as she was ugly" (197, 198). And "Swedes" (who get the xenophobic treatment from nearly all the Bunyan authors) are childish and stupid. And "bohunks" (*Dictionary of American Slang*: "An immigrant from central or eastern Europe...a stupid, clumsy person; lout") are worthless as workers. And forests are incidentally "logged off," and Paul "did all sorts of crazy things to the animals of the North Woods" (169).

But (and that's starting to look like a pretty indefensible "but") the primary intent of Shay's Bunyan stories is humor, and quite a lot of them are actually funny:

As a teen-logger, "Paul was sensitive about his height and did all he could to discourage attempts to find out how big he was. Once he caught some civil engineers with their transit leveled on him. What he did to those engineers and chainmen was not what could be called civil" (168).

Prior to Paul's invention of the grindstone, "the axmen used to sharpen their tools by rolling rocks down hill and running alongside of them. It took an axman seven days to properly sharpen his ax and the waste of time, when you stop to think they had to be sharpened every other day, was something awful" (172).

Before Paul hitches Babe to an especially curvy road to straighten it out, it is "as crooked as a Philadelphia politician" (176). After the job is completed, it is "as straight as the path of rectitude" (180).

When Billy Puget tries to cheat Paul out of the money coming to him for digging Puget Sound and Paul, in revenge, starts filling it back in (creating the San Juan Islands), Puget's "lawyer fellow began yelling 'Mandamus, habeas corpus, corpus delicti, precedent, lease, cease, stop and desist' and a whole lot of other gibberage but old Paul went right on throwing the dirt back" (218).

So can we (excepting the lawyers, of course) forgive Shay for the earlier affronts? You decide.

○

(Still trying to do that summary...)

Glen Rounds' *Ol' Paul, the Mighty Logger* (1936) is perhaps the "classic" children's Paul Bunyan book. It's the one that Hoffman, in 1952, likes the most, and it's probably the one that many of us baby-boomers checked out from our elementary school libraries. The inside book jacket flap of my 1976 "40th Anniversary Edition" (another used-book Internet acquisition; I live a good distance from those 10,000-plus Library of Congress holdings) states that the book has been continuously in print since the date of its original publication – continuously in print until 1976, that is – and gives us approving review-blurbs from the *Library Journal*, *The New York Times*, and *The Dallas News*. And – though by now you've probably figured out that I'm not too keen on His Lordship Paul Bunyan – it's a delightful little book, and someone needs to re-issue it.

Daniel Hoffman longs for a writer of Mark Twain's stature to give us a Paul-Bunyan-as-National-Epic-Hero, and thank God Twain stuck to Huck.

Rounds takes Bunyan in the only direction ethically possible – into all-out preposterous humor, with a dash of satire – and if Rounds had had the first and last word on Bunyan, I wouldn't be writing this essay.

There are laughs on every page:

[No one knows Babe's exact size.] However, they tell of an eagle that had been in the habit of roosting on the tip of Babe's right horn, suddenly deciding to fly to the other. Columbus Day, it was, when he started. He flew steadily, so they say, night and day, fair weather and foul, until his wing feathers were worn down to pinfeathers and a new set grew to replace them. In all, he seems to have worn out seventeen sets of feathers on the trip, and from reaching up to brush the sweat out of his eyes so much, had worn all the feathers off the top of his head, becoming completely bald, as are all of his descendants to this day. Finally the courageous bird won through, reaching the brass ball on the tip of the left horn on the seventeenth of March. He waved a wing weakly at the cheering lumberjacks and 'lowed as how he'd of made it sooner but for the head winds (19).

As everyone knows, most bunkhouses have a certain number of bedbugs... [These] intelligent little beasts always knew when camp was to be moved, and the night before would come out of wherever they were in the habit of staying and climb into the bedding rolls so as not to be left behind. Then when the new camp was set up, there they were, jumping up and down with excitement to greet the men when they came in from their first day's work (27-28).

At that time there were no figures as we know them now. So [Paul] has to do all his figuring in his head and keep all his records there too. It takes eight days and forty-seven hours to figure the payroll alone, and that's only the beginning... His fingers get blistered from counting on them, but he doesn't stop, and new blisters form and push the old ones back towards his wrists, and still he keeps on counting. Finally the tips of his fingers are blistered clear to his elbows (64-65). [So eventually Paul finds master-figurer Johnny Inkslinger.]And the fellow seems to be a real artist, so probably could be hired for practically nothing (72).

And no racism, no sexism, no chauvinism, no xenophobia, no worker-bashing, no monopolist-capitalist idolatry, no "Superhero" Paul...and, wonder of wonders, no smugly superior attitude toward the natural world.

Come on, it's 1936! What's wrong with this guy?

(Okay, I give up on the summary. But only four more books to go. Fast. I promise.)

Dell J. McCormick came out with two Bunyan books three years apart – *Paul Bunyan Swings His Axe* in 1936, and *Tall Timber Tales* in '39. They're aimed at a younger, less sophisticated children's audience than is Rounds' book (or maybe Rounds just didn't write down to the kids), and the second one is a *little* better, a *little* looser than the first, but they're both just basically boring. Plus, the same old horsehockey: "wonderful forests" that exist only to be cut down, rivers and animals that must be "tamed" and killed respectively, and the matter-of-fact observation that "The great forests are no more" (*Tall* 153).

But! "The spirit of Paul Bunyan lives on in America," (155) McCormick assures the fourth-graders in the last paragraph of his second book, so we can be happy about that.

We get the woman's touch again (sorry, women, if that sounds a mite condescending; this macho Bunyan stuff is starting to grow on me) in Anne Malcolmson's 1941 compilation *Yankee Doodle's Cousins*. She writes, in her Preface to the book, of the "need [in children] for an awareness of democracy and its blessings...in these tragic days" (vii).

Fine. No argument. It's 1941. And I'm already starting to feel like a heel for what I'm about to say.

However, when we get to Paul Bunyan, who's awarded his own introduction and the last three chapters of the book (each of the other folk heroes rates just one), we're told that "all Yankee Doodle's Cousins" consider Paul their "lord and master" and that Paul is the "patron saint" of "Real Americans" (229).

Democracy?

No, more James Stevens trash.

It's amazing the extent to which these Paul Bunyan writers plagiarize the pants off one another. (Not Rounds. He borrows a few broad outlines, then creates new material of his own.) Malcolmson's whole first Bunyan chapter is lifted straight out of Stevens, with the same "Superpatriotic" denouement: after struggling endlessly to decipher the meaning of these mysterious dreams he's been having, Paul decides "He had to go to Real America and invent logging" (239), blah blah blah. Forget humor. Forget irony. Just re-hashed Stevens for two more chapters. Not food I wish to consume.

Finally...well, let's end this discussion of the early children's Bunyan books on a positive note: Walter Blair, author of the 1944 compilation *Tall Tale America*, illustrated by Glen Rounds, whose scratchy, unromanticized pen-and-ink drawings enhanced his own book. Blair takes a page out of Rounds (fairly) and goes from there.

Unlike Malcolmson's/Steven's Bunyan, who "invents logging" without the author's apparently ever realizing the peculiarity of inventing something for which a word already exists, Blair's Bunyan invents things right and left that *Bunyan* may not know have been sitting in our dictionaries for quite some time but that Blair's young readers do.

"Guess I'll invent a grindstone... Here's a Two-Man Saw I invented... Guess I'll invent a round-turn..." (168, 169, 170).

Other quick takes:

Paul's a "Scientific Industrialist, in a nice way" (167). What? You mean not all Scientific Industrialists are nice?

Babe "could haul logs to the landing quicker than a scandal could travel" (171).

In order to wake the sound-sleeping lumberjacks in the morning, "the Bull Cook would take the baton that Big Swede Ole had made and would pound the big triangle with it until the echoes got going every which way, bumped into one another, and started to wrestle. This made such a huge and interesting din that everybody piled out immediately or even sooner" (181-182).

And Paul is first attracted to his future wife when he sees her rescuing her sister from being swept over a falls by "uproot[ing] trees and cliffs and fling[ing] them into the water – not the way a woman usually does, awkward and sprawly, but overhand..." (177).

Now, not even I – touchy me – can find fault with that.

O

So it's the closing decades of the twentieth century, and for some unfathomable reason you've decided to add your name to that 10,000-plus list. What kinds of problems are you facing?

Well, bashing blacks is uncool. Bashing women is uncool. Bashing foreigners is mostly uncool. And you've *really* got a problem in the fact that Paul Bunyan's occupation is obliterating whole ecosystems.

What to do?

The answer most of them seem to have come up with is to turn Paul Bunyan into a kind of not-Paul Bunyan, a "What, me a logger?" Alfred E. Neuman-type Paul Bunyan.

No more stern countenance a la Shay's book. And the fiendish look that Rockwell Kent gave him? Out of the question. Instead, everyone's happy, even the soon-to-be-exterminated animals. On the cover of popular children's author/illustrator Steven Kellogg's 1984 *Paul Bunyan* (Amazon. com's average customer rating for this book is five stars), there sits Paul in the midst of a pristine wilderness, happy mountain lions crawling all over him like kittens, happy Babe smiling over his left shoulder, a happy bald eagle (U.S. mascot) smiling over his right. (Paul, though he sports a beard, looks to be about ten years old.) Open the book...and no one seems able to contain their joy. Everything is sweetness and light – people and nature co-existing in perfect harmony. Last page...why, of course...a whole *family* of smiling bald eagles, one alighting smilingly on a smiling Paul Bunyan's finger, Babe looking on smilingly from behind.

Animal killing is way down in the later books, even imaginary-animal killing, perhaps because most animals other than dogs and cats are "imaginary" to most Americans anyway. In a 1966 compilation entitled *American Tall Tales* by Adrien Stoutenburg, Paul at one point kills "thousands of wild ducks," but accidentally, and "Paul felt sorry for the ducks, but there was nothing to do but gather them up and hand them over to the cooks" (18). In other treatments, animals like the Gumberoos have to be really, really bad to merit retaliation against them.

The "Oh, how sweet" factor is frequently played up, like Paul as an infant innocently flattening whole stands of "timber" when he rolls over, and Paul rescuing and nurturing back to health the baby ox Babe during the Winter of the Blue Snow.

Certain elements like Babe pulling the impossibly-curvy logging road straight and the corn stalk that won't stop growing ("Jack in the Beanstalk" revisited) seem safe enough and so are regularly repeated. Also, that giant pancake griddle. I got a kick out of Kellogg's illustration of the scene: in it, we've come all the way from "coons" and "darkey cookboys" greasing the griddle to white guys doing all the work with the exception of...the one token black.

And trees?

Well, we get less and less specific mention of Michigan, Wisconsin, and Minnesota being "logged off" and more and more exclusive focus on the imaginary Onion River and Round River country. The logging-off of North Dakota is still a staple – but how many kids, I wonder, especially our current computer-game-Internet-mesmerized batch (if they even read anymore) get that joke?

Fairly common, though more cursory than the one below, are semi-apologetic passages like the following (from Mary Pope Osborne's 1991 compilation *American Tall Tales*):

> In those times, huge sections of America were filled with dark green forests. And the forests were filled with trees – oceans of trees – trees as far as the eye could see – trees so tall you had to look straight up to see if it was morning, and maybe if you were lucky, you'd catch a glimpse of blue sky.
>
> It would be nice if those trees could have stayed tall and thick forever. But the pioneers needed them to build houses, churches, ships, wagons, bridges, and barns. So one day Paul Bunyan took a good look at all those trees and said, "Babe, stand back. I'm about to invent logging" (103).

But I don't want to seem to be criticizing Osborne because, in the Introduction to her book, she also says this:

> As I combed through old material to select which yarns to retell, I found it disheartening to come across stories that derided African Americans, Native Americans, women, and animals. And considering our environmental problems today, I was less than enthusiastic about the goal of conquering the wilderness at all costs. Therefore, I decided I would attempt to bring out the more vulnerable and compassionate side of the tall-tale characters in my retellings. I sought to revitalize the stories' essential spirit of gargantuan physical courage and absurd humor, de-emphasizing incidents that would seem cruel or insensitive to today's readers (xi).

Okay, laudable sentiment, but it's just, it's just...well, I don't know that her goal, in the case of our "Greatest American Superhero," is achievable.

○

One other element of the Bunyan stories that persists into the present (and into my step-daughter's third-grade social studies text) is Paul Bunyan's creation of geography – the Mississippi, the Rocky Mountains, the Great Lakes, the Grand Canyon, and so on.

Seems harmless enough. Right?

For an answer, let's look at some American Indian "tall tales."

Everyone knows that the aboriginal American-Indian view of the natural world was much different (to understate things just a tad) from the Judeo-Christian/European-American/Frontier-Mentality view: humans as a part *of* and coequal with the natural world, instead of apart *from* and superior to it. That's easy enough to state (I just managed it in nineteen words), and easy to speechify about, but to truly understand it in a *deep* sense, to *know* it without having to "understand" it, to possess that knowing in your being as well as your brain – that, surely, is impossible for any "Modern," most modern American Indians included. We can respect it. We can desire it. We can, willingly or grudgingly, consent to its truth. (And lately, in a negative way, we're being forced to consent to its truth, aren't we? – with global climate change now a generally recognized fact; with the population of *homo sapiens* on this planet at 6.5 billion and increasing by 10 million, net, every month and a half; and with, ecologists now believe, the first *human*-caused mass extinction of species in this planet's history now in full swing.) But we can't assume that it can be understood in the way, for example, that the causes of World War II can be understood, and it would be monumentally presumptuous of us to think otherwise.

Many American Indian myths and legends are infused with this view of humans-as-part- of-nature. They are not "tall tales" (Indians have their tall tales also): they are "true." They're the *Bible*, the *Torah*, the *Koran*, and maybe, with the fix we've gotten our little floating ball into, they're proving "truer" than all those other three tomes combined.

People in these myths do not create geography, or have "dominion" over the earth, or "subdue" it, or "name" the animals; their role in the Big Broad Scheme of Things is much more humble. Sometimes they are descended from animals (as, of course, we are): the Modoc are descended from grizzlies, the Brule Sioux from the eagle, and they think of rattlesnakes as their cousins. People and animals in these stories can talk to one another, they intermarry, and animals are forever helping people and teaching them things. Sometimes animals *are* people, and vice versa. In a Snohomish story, people and animals work together to push up the sky, which the Creator has made so low that "tall people bumped their heads against it" (Erdoes 96). (The Creator or Great Spirit or Sky Spirit or Old Man of the Ancients – he has many names – is no Yahweh; sometimes he screws up.) In a Shasta story, Ground Squirrel steals the first arrowheads from Obsidian Old Man and gives them to the people. In a Crow story Old Man Coyote makes the world, including people, and then gives the people weapons with which to hunt. In a White Mountain Apache story, Turkey gives the people corn and then shows them how to grow it, and Bear gives them acorns, various forms of edible cacti, pinon nuts, and different kinds of berries. In a Kwakiutl story, animals teach people how to dance.

People creating geography? Not hardly. That's more of your white-man-arrogance stuff.

O

Poor ol' Paul. We've got to bring an end to our stories about him somehow. What should we do? Kill him off, leave him hanging, keep him going?

The consensus, from Esther Shephard in 1924 all the way up to the present, is that we keep him going. Most of the books end with Paul, having completed his work in the lower forty-eight, heading off with Babe into the "far North" or the "wilderness" or the "deep woods" or Alaska (oil-rich, timber-rich, conservationist-poor Alaska is the favorite), with assurances that he's still up-there/out-there somewhere keeping that American Spirit alive.

And that's appropriate, don't you think?

Because... Well, look at it this way... Because as long as "progress" and money and "We have to" keep ol' Mother Nature (even older than Paul, I'd guess) sweating away at that second fiddle; as long as we consider it not only our right *but our duty!* to be fruitful and multiply; as long as we fail to make the connection, or ignore it, between the way we live and the ecological crisis we're creating – not just the SUV's and the faux mansion-houses in the farmland-housing-developments, but all the wasteful glossy packaging of all the "merchandise" we don't need, all the electronic garbage, all the computerized junk (wait...you mean it takes energy and natural resources to produce and use that stuff? we aren't getting it from Mars or someplace?); as long as the American Dream means little more than "Let's produce/buy/ consume whatever our engineers and business executives can conjure up... because we can afford it!" (4.5% of the world's population – consumption of 25% of its resources); as long as we try to mollify ourselves with the fond wish that the Government or the Sierra Club will fix things for us; as long as we can see no value in simplicity and reflection and restraint...

...Yes, Paul Bunyan lives.

Sources

Blair, Walter. *Tall Tale America*. New York: Coward-McCann, 1944.

Bonnicksen, Thomas M. *America's Ancient Forests: From the Ice Age to the Age of Discovery*. New York: John Wiley & Sons, Inc., 2000.

Brown, Nelson C. *Logging: The Principles and Methods of Harvesting Timber in the United States and Canada*. New York: John Wiley & Sons, Inc., 1934.

Cokinos, Christopher. *Hope Is the Thing With Feathers*. New York: Jeremy P. Tarcher/Putnam, 2000.

Davis, Mary Byrd, ed. *Eastern Old-Growth Forests: Prospects for Rediscovery and Recovery*. Washington, D.C.: Island Press,1996.

Dorson, Richard M. *Folklore and Fakelore: Essays Toward a Discipline of Folk Studies*. Cambridge, MA: Harvard UP, 1976.

Erdoes, Richard and Alfonso Ortiz, eds. *American Indian Myths and Legends*. New York: Pantheon Books, 1984.

Felton, Harold W., ed. *Legends of Paul Bunyan*. New York: Knopf, 1947.

Flader, Susan L., ed. *The Great Lakes Forest: An Environmental and Social History*. Minneapolis: University of Minnesota Press, 1983.

Fries, Robert F. *Empire in Pine: The Story of Lumbering in Wisconsin 1830-1900*. Ellison Bay, WI: Wm Caxton Ltd, 1951.

Hoffman, Daniel. *Paul Bunyan: Last of the Frontier Demigods*. New York: Temple University Publications, 1952.

Jensen, Vernon H. *Lumber and Labor*. New York: Farrar & Rinehart, 1945.

Kellogg, Steven. *Paul Bunyan*. New York: Mulberry, 1984.

MacGillivray, James. "The Round River Drive." *Legends of Paul Bunyan*. Ed. Harold W. Felton. New York: Knopf, 1947.

Malcolmson, Anne. *Yankee Doodle's Cousins*. Boston: Houghton Mifflin, 1941.

Malloch, Douglas. "The Round River Drive." *Legends of Paul Bunyan*. Ed. Harold W. Felton.New York: Knopf, 1947.

McCormick, Dell J. *Paul Bunyan Swings His Axe*. New York: The Caxton Printers, Ltd.., 1936.

—. *Tall Timber Tales*. Caldwell, ID: The Caxton Printers, 1966 [c1939].

Osborne, Mary Pope. *American Tall Tales*. New York: Knopf, 1991.

Rounds, Glen. *Ol' Paul, The Mighty Logger*. New York: Holiday House, 1976.

Shay, Frank. *Here's Audacity!* New York: The Macaulay Co., 1930.

Shephard, Esther. *Paul Bunyan*. New York: Harcourt, Brace & Co., 1924.

Stevens, James. *Paul Bunyan*. Garden City, NY: Garden City Publishing Co., Inc., 1925.

—. *The Saginaw Paul Bunyan*. Detroit: Wayne State University Press, 1987.

Stoutenburg, Adrien. *American Tall Tales*. New York: Viking, 1966.

Wadsworth, Wallace. *Paul Bunyan and His Great Blue Ox*. Garden City, NY: Doubleday & Co., Inc., 1964 [c1926].

The Reed

*E*l Tule is anything but.

Spanish for "the reed," El Tule is a tree – a Montezuma Baldcypress to be exact, *Taxodium mucronatum* to be more exact – whose trunk has the largest girth, 58 meters, of any tree in the world. At 42 meters high, El Tule is also very tall, but its sheer size (estimated weight: 636,000+ tons) is what amazes. Standing next to it is like standing at the base of a cliff. Above, the massive branches carve twisting canyons out of the sky.

The tree is also, with two to three millennia under its belt, one of the world's oldest, and is said to have been worshiped by the Zapotecs, who were conquered by the Mixtecs, who in turn were conquered by the Aztecs, as the god of growth. It dwarfs both in size and in age the 17th century Spanish mission that sits behind it, and is by far the largest "structure," along with seven other somewhat less imposing siblings, in the small pueblo, Santa Maria del Tule, that features the tree as its main tourist attraction. An annual El Tule Festival is held each October, and the tree can even boast its own society, Mi Amigo el Arbol, whose self-appointed charge it is to look after El Tule, whose future is in jeopardy because of the shrinking aquifer below.

Santa Maria del Tule is in Oaxaca, Mexico's penultimate southernmost state. Famous for its rich and varied cuisine, its cultural diversity (sixteen indigenous peoples), its handicrafts, its pre-Columbian archeological sites, its mountainous terrain, and its spring-like year-round climate, Oaxaca draws tourists from all over the world.

Oaxaca is also famous, though probably not among tourists, as one of the most deforested and desertified regions on earth. Its mountains, according to a U.N. report, are "the most eroded landscape on the planet" (Simon 35); huge portions of its once-arable land are now ruined; and the poverty of its people – some of the poorest in Mexico – isn't helping matters any.

Poverty has a long history in Mexico, and it is closely tied to the land. Under Spanish colonial law, Indians had the theoretical right to a small amount of land for growing subsistence-level corn, beans, and squash (their staple foods), but this "right" tended to clash with the Spanish settlers' notion that the land – made even more abundant than it already was by European diseases that wiped out up to 90% of the Indian population – was theirs for the taking. The settlers' cattle, introduced in 1520, did the bulk of the taking: they reproduced like rabbits on fertility drugs, overran and gobbled up the Indians' crops, and forced entire villages to pack up and leave in a futile attempt to escape the hoofed vermin. As the Indians were driven off their land, the Spanish settlers' estates mysteriously grew, and then generous offers of "employment" were made to the Indians.

By the time Mexico secured its independence from Spain in 1821, these landed estates (or haciendas) had grown to enormous proportions, and the peasantry's plight had grown steadily worse. Attempts were made at reform – most notably by Oaxaca-born president Benito Juárez, whose efforts in the late 1850s were aimed at a more equitable redistribution of land – but colonialism had simply morphed into neocolonialism, and the entrenched aristocracy stood its ground. The long and messy Mexican Revolution – whose battle cry was "Land to those who work it!" – did produce the Constitution of 1917, whose famous Article 27 at least gave lip service to "a more equitable distribution of wealth" by declaring that all land and natural resources were the property of the state, but "Let's give everyone a piece of the pie" was an idealistic goal, not a guarantee. When land reform finally did arrive in the 1930s under president Lázaro Cárdenas, with Article 27 as its legal basis, it was not a response to a call for fairness and justice but a political and economic ploy: dole out millions of acres of (mostly non-hacienda) land to the rural peasants, who will produce lots of cheap food for Mexico's urban industrial workers, who then can be paid lower wages to help finance industrial growth...and when the next "election" rolls around, with all those rural peasants lodged securely in your pockets, get re-elected.

This, along with ballot-stuffing and other indelicate practices, is how Mexico's dominant political party, the Institutional Revolutionary Party (PRI), stayed in power for over sixty years. The problem was that most of the land parceled out, by Cárdenas and subsequently, was marginal at best or not farmland at all, a full three-fourths being either forested or suitable only for grazing cattle (Simon 41). So when, enjoined by the federal government to produce food for a national market, the peasant farmers tried to oblige, a cycle of failure was set in motion: they pushed their land to its cultivatable limits, ended up exhausting it, cleared more marginal land, ended up exhausting that, and then either returned to subsistence farming or, finding even that impossible (deforestation, especially on mountain slopes, leading inevitably to erosion), fled to the cities.

The so-called Green Revolution in the 1950s and '60s, and its adherents' blind faith in technological fixes, was intended to stop this downward spiral and usher Mexico (and India, and other "developing" countries) into a wondrous new agricultural future. Wonderful pesticides like DDT, wonderful fertilizers, wonderful new seed varieties, would increase yields, end rural poverty, and put Mexico on the global economic map. The PRI-controlled government, ever mindful of keeping the peasantry dependent upon its beneficence, offered farmers fertilizers and pesticides at subsidized rates, and at first even the marginal lands produced corn like they had been born again in Iowa. But then the cycle of failure returned: after a few years, crop yields declined to pre-chemicals levels, necessitating more chemicals – and then more – while at the same time the government subsidies stopped, necessitating loans from government banks – and then more loans – until land and peasants alike were ruined.

This broken record continued to play until 1992 when...it continued to play some more. In that year, Article 27 was amended, bringing an end to land reform, on the grounds, first of all, that there was no more land left to give away, and second, that large-scale agricultural production was economically preferable to "inefficient" small-scale production. Also, the North American Free Trade Agreement (NAFTA) was in the works, and the effective repeal of Article 27 was expected to harmonize nicely with NAFTA's bouncy globalization refrain.

The land that the Mexican government had distributed for sixty years under Article 27 had always come with strings attached. Technically, the government still owned it. Peasants could farm the land – in fact, were required to farm the land – and could leave it as an inheritance of sorts, but could not rent, sell, or mortgage it, which of course kept them firmly stuck in poverty. These stipulations, along with subsidies and various forms of arm-twisting, had worked to keep the peasantry where the government wanted it – in a habitual state of dependency and obligation – but had also kept Mexican agriculture out of the world's markets. It was hoped that with the "reform" of land reform (peasants now *could* sell their land), big-money agri-business consolidation would take charge, Mexican agriculture would enter the global economy, and the peasants, those sacrificial lambs of modernization...well, they'd just have to fend for themselves.

But it didn't happen. Instead, for various reasons scholars continue to discuss – widespread disregard of Article 27's stipulations in the first place; a strong fealty even to marginal land until circumstances compel flight; economic recession – the cycle of failure, like the medieval wheel of fortune, grinds on. Today, U.S. politicians carp about our illegal immigration problem (which NAFTA didn't, as promised, solve but made worse, by requiring Mexican farmers to compete with their American and Canadian counterparts), and offer as solutions racist legislation and Berlin Wall-style border fences, conveniently forgetting that problems, generally speaking, are preceded by causes. Yes, the causes of this particular problem are deep and complex, far deeper and more complex than my little synopsis here could possibly have conveyed, but any peasant Mexican farmer could sum them up for any fatuous U.S. senator even more concisely than have I, in one simple sentence: "The land no longer gives."

○

The land no longer gives.

Perhaps the land no longer gives for the impoverished Mexican farmer, and will in time no longer give in all the ways we've come to expect for all the rest of us, because all we do as humans is take. Political hegemony in Mexico, corporate greed in America, industrial "progress" in China – the motives may differ (or do they?), but the end result is always the same: the "land," and the land's poorest occupants, paying the highest price. Deforestation, erosion, melting icecaps, dying seas – just the "cost" of keeping those of us currently alive currently happy. That big tree in that tiny Mexican village *is* a reed – like all the sad, frail remnants of the natural world that will be left once humans have had their fill: a cypress clinging to life in the middle of a human-produced desert, straining nourishment from a human-depleted aquifer below, and oh-so-cherished by the humans who come to visit.

Sources

Gledhill, John. "Fantasy and Reality in Restructuring Mexico's Land Reform." Paper presented to the "Modern Mexico" session of the annual meeting of the Society for Latin American Studies, St. Andrews, Scotland, 6 April 1997. (Internet source.)

Goldsborough, James O. "Farm Problems Expose Weak Link of NAFTA." *San Diego Union Tribune*. 2 Jan. 2003.

Luers, Amy L., Rosamond L. Naylor, and Pamela A. Matson. "A Case Study of Land Reform and Coastal Land Transformation in Southern Sonora, Mexico." Center for Environmental Science and Policy, Stanford University. (Internet source.)

Magaloni, Beatriz, Barry Weingast, and Alberto Diaz-Cayeros. "Why Authoritarian Regimes Sabotage Economic Growth: Land Reform in Mexico." Center on Democracy, Development, and the Rule of Law, Stanford University. (Internet source.)

Quintana, Roberto Diego, Luciano Concheiro Bórquez, and Ricardo Pérez Aviles. "Peasant Logic, Agrarian Policy, Land Mobility, and Land Markets in Mexico." Land Tenure Center, University of Wisconsin – Madison. (Internet source.)

Simon, Joel. *Endangered Mexico*. San Francisco: Sierra Club Books, 1997.

THREE:

HIGH AND DRY

Desert Ships

*T*he agave or century plant (*Agave neomexicana*) is a yucca-like plant of the Chihuahuan Desert that reaches its northern range of growth in southwest Texas and southern New Mexico. Though it does resemble several species of desert plants we commonly lump together under the term "yucca" (Wheeler sotol, soaptree yucca, Spanish dagger, etc.), the agave is a member of the amaryllis family while yuccas belong – not surprisingly when you see the flowers – to the lily family. Like a yucca, the agave is comprised of a mass of spear-like leaves that radiate up and outward from its base, and its flowers are produced at the top of a long stalk or scape that rises vertically from the center of the plant. Its toothed leaves, however, are much wider and pulpier than a yucca's, and are closer to blue than green and edged in black. Though the thickness of the leaves makes them look as if they would be spongy to the touch, they are in fact leather-tough and rigid as wood. In general the agave is a more obdurate, more menacing-looking plant than most yuccas. You would never make the mistake of brushing past an agave as you might the flimsier sotol unless you wanted to risk impaling your leg on one of its iron-hard, lance-like, toxin-tipped spines.

The agave's forbidding, perdurable appearance is appearance only, however, for it flowers just once and then abruptly dies. It reaches an age of between eight and twenty years (not a hundred), sends up its first and last flower stalk in the final season of its life, blossoms, produces seeds, and leaves behind a sprinkling of small agaves growing about its withering base. The flower stalk can ascend to a height of fifteen feet, and grows at a remarkable rate of speed, often several inches a day. It is as if the plant is in a race against time to produce its offspring before it dies, sometimes appearing to be in the process of dying even as it sends up its stalk, as if it is channeling the last vestiges of its life out of its graying leaves and into that shoot, or as if in defiance of all logic it is determined to become most alive at the exact moment of its demise. The frothy yellow flower-clusters burst forth from their red casings on finger-like projections that look like hands upturned as if in supplication or offering, each finger sprouting flowers from its tip. The sight of these plants in all their splendor is a stirring one, their stalks as prominent on the desert horizon as the masts of ships, each plant brandishing its colors as a glorious prelude to its death, reserving for its final moments its greatest achievement.

My wife and I did some hiking this last summer in the Guadalupe Mountains of southwest Texas, where we saw a lot of agaves. The Guadalupe Mountains are themselves a unique natural phenomenon, formed from an ancient fossil reef laid down in the Permian Age, the largest such reef in the world. In more recent geologic times, these mountains were covered, as was much of West Texas, with a vast coniferous forest that disappeared with the end of the last ice age and the warmer, drier climate that followed – disappeared, that is, from all of West Texas except the upper slopes of the Guadalupes, where it remains as a remnant of its former self, surrounded on all sides by desert. Today the Guadalupes shelter a rich and unusual mix of plants and animals that reach the geographic limits of their range within the mountain's borders – agaves and sotols from the Chihuahuan Desert growing next to Douglas fir and ponderosa pine from the Rockies, Texas madrone from Mexico sharing the same soil with the eastern chinquapin oak.

One thing that struck me about the agaves I saw on our backpacking trip was that many of those that were growing beside the trail had had their flower stalks broken off. Those that were growing at a distance from the trail were undisturbed; only the plants within easy reach had been molested. Apparently hikers, seeing perhaps in the agave's flower stalk a fancy walking stick, which they would have immediately realized is unsatisfactory for such a purpose, being both too large and too light, were the culprits, having broken off the stalks in the process of their flowering and so preventing the plants from staging their final display.

This was not, I'd like to make clear, a nature trail we were hiking, one of those blacktopped, half-mile loops for the faint of heart and flabby of belly, but a rough, steep backcountry trail in a wilderness area, miles of rocky plodding from any campground or road, miles too, you would think, from the sort of mentality that would beget such an act. During one stretch of four days, we encountered only one other pair of hikers, and when we returned a ranger informed me that the four of us had been the only people making use of the trails. Plus, in the Guadalupes, in addition to everything else in your pack, you must also tote your own water, there being no perennial streams, so you do not get to see those agaves without a considerable expense of effort, and it isn't your typical car-bound tourist that you expect to find in such a place, but a person who you'd think would have developed a fairly fine-tuned sense of appreciation for the natural world, slow and hard as his progress through it is.

I live in the city like everyone else, and drive my car that pollutes the air, and contribute my share of garbage to the nation's landfills, but I have to confess to a certain bafflement as to why someone would knock over an agave's flower stalk at the peak of its glory. It doesn't finally matter, I suppose, that the agave's life cycle is cut short with the stalk – except to the extent that it is thereby prevented from reproducing. The plant cannot lament what has been done to it, is incapable of feeling anger or pain at being denied its chance to fulfill its genetic mission. It's, after all, only a plant. Still, why isn't it possible just to leave the thing alone? If a walking stick is what they wanted, why didn't they bring one from home or find a piece of deadwood lying around? If they were itching to get a closer look at the flowers, why didn't they climb a nearby ledge and make an adventure of their looking? If they didn't know that an agave does not flower many times but only once, why didn't they know, and why should not knowing make any difference?

Perhaps those frothy yellow offerings to the sky were just so pretty they couldn't bear not to destroy them.

Desert ships run aground on human reefs.

Laughing Gulls and Chameleons

*S*outh Texas, unless you reside on the coast – and by that I mean within three or four miles of the water – is not a very agreeable place to live. It is dirt-dry and insufferably humid at the same time – a "desert jungle," as someone has said, the humidity coming not from out of the sky but from off the Gulf – and is either hot, fairly hot, or extremely hot depending on the time of year. Winter-like weather does sometimes occur, but it is short-lived and sporadic, and the trees that had finally lost their leaves by around Christmas are already budding again by late January. Fall is just a slightly less humid extension of summer, and spring a similar extension from the other end. Spring also brings gritty, near gale-force winds raking without cease across the landscape – which are nothing, of course, compared to the occasional hurricane served up by summer.

Extreme South Texas is as flat as a becalmed sea, having once been covered by a sea itself, and is largely treeless except for mesquite, the few live oak that are left, and the non-native palms that people plant. Droughts can last, not months or seasons, but years; lawns and gardens burn up with predictable regularity; and fifty-percent yields of the region's cotton and sorghum crops are so common that one is moved to ask, "Fifty percent of what?" Texas-sized roaches, your cleanliness notwithstanding, will have the run of your place without regular visits from the bug man; fleas, pets or no pets, are a menace every spring; and those harmless-looking little fire ants will turn the simple act of stepping across your yard into a Hindu fire-walking ritual. The region's two principal cities, Corpus Christi and Brownsville, are worthy of note – Corpus for its bayfront and Brownsville for its border – but most of South Texas is unremittingly rural, and without, say, the picturesqueness of New England or the quaint dilapidation of East Tennessee.

I lived in South Texas for four years and do not, as you may have gathered, much miss it, but two components of my former home do come back to me with a kind of sheen around my thoughts of them: laughing gulls and chameleons.

I don't know why these two creatures reside so happily in my memory, why them and no others, why animals at all and not people-matters of some sort (the richness of the Hispanic culture in South Texas, for example) – all I know is that they do. When I think of them I smile, and the affection I feel for them in retrospect is greater than my regard for them at the time. Maybe it's what I see as their essentially comical nature, their peculiar array of quirky rituals and exertions, or maybe it's something else. At any rate, whenever I think back to my sojourn in Texas, it's laughing gulls and chameleons that come to mind.

All gulls, my reading informs me, are noisy (the need to be heard over that surf), but it is laughing gulls that raise the level of their noisy calls to a raucous art. They are called "laughing" because of the ostensibly ha-ha-ha-ha-*haah-haah-haah-haah* nature of their outbursts, but if laughter this is, then it is laughter of which one would not wish to be the target, for it is particularly high-pitched, screechy, and aggressive, definitely more *at* its object than *with*, and bristling with chest-thumping self-assertiveness, intolerance, and rebuke. It is leveled at any and all comers, for reasons manifest and obscure, and can suddenly erupt among a group of formerly quiet birds, everyone shouting at once, everyone miffed. It is subject to numerous variations in intensity and length, from obligatory time-to-pop-off-again to outright fury, while retaining its same basic pattern – a series of short, staccato squawks followed by longer, louder shrieks – from bird to bird. It is brash, indignant, mocking, bumptious, arrogant, and wild – the call of a bird that knows the world is its oyster. The first distinctive thing you're likely to notice about this gull, often before you see it, and the last thing you'll forget, is its call.

Gulls seem to have three main interests in life – food, territory, and a kind of farcical obsession with being noticed – and their calls give expression to all three needs. The mad, wheeling air-show that results when a flock of birds gives chase to one of their number who has managed to secure a scrap of anything at all is accompanied by squawks that say, "That-food-you-have-should-be-*mine-mine-mine-mine-mine!*" and when a younger or less aggressive gull attempts a landing near one of his betters, he is greeted with a neck-extended, "Get-a-way-from-me-*now-now-now-now-now!*" Sometimes a gull flying alone above his comrades will cut loose with a string of squawks whose only apparent purpose is to proclaim, "Look-at-me-you-fools-I'm-*here-here-here-here-here!*" At other times a bird of this ilk who can't seem to keep his beak shut when his companions would prefer quiet will be turned on with a jab and a resounding, "Your-rack-et-is-mak-ing-me-*mad-mad-*

mad-mad-mad!" Except when the call is unleashed in flight, it is frequently punctuated with one last squawk set apart from the rest by a slight pause and a theatrical toss of the head to the sky. "So there!" says the gesture, leaving the impression that nothing more need be said – until, of course, something more does need to be said, in another half minute or so.

Despite their habitual nastiness toward one another – the selfishness, the greed, the insistence on occupying *this* gull's piling when another, unoccupied one is just a few feet away – gulls are actually quite gregarious and hang around together, not just during breeding season, but throughout the year. One sees them lined up in perfect formation – always facing out to sea – along jetties and breakwaters; standing together in clusters on park lawns or atop bath-houses; or sitting like ducks in the marina at low tide. They are capable of periods of relatively squabble-free harmony – horizon-gazing, feather-grooming, gull-type peaceful moments – and the disputes that do break out are often resolved quickly, with a round of squawks and a couple of jabs with the beak. A given assembly of gulls, if left undisturbed, may stay together for several hours, individual birds coming and going, larger factions occasionally taking off in pursuit of a shrimp boat or a rival with a fish, newcomers taking their place, either circling in for a landing from above and dropping softly into a single, vacant spot (always alighting facing the exact same direction as the group), or gliding in low and straight from behind like an airplane and waddling to a stop, the others clucking a greeting, anyone who shows up apparently welcome. Over time the group will collectively shift forward into the wind as a natural consequence of the birds individually righting themselves against gusts, intensifying the impression of avian unity. Then a tourist will blunder by or an eager child will rush at the birds, and with a sudden flurry of gray-white flapping wings, they're off.

Laughing gulls are clearly not the kind of bird to which one is moved to attach high-sounding adjectives, but in flight, if not in repose, they are truly impressive. Standing around on the ground on their spindly, knobby-kneed black legs, their webbed feet reducing what little walking they attempt to a comical waddle, their black-hooded heads like under-sized hats, they resemble nothing so much as small, feathery Charlie Chaplins turning this way and that in dim confusion. It is not the sort of sight that coaxes odes from impassioned breasts, but get a laughing gull into the air and he'll draw your respect. They are agile, even acrobatic, fliers, able to turn and feint on a dime, to hover in mid-air in a way that recalls a hummingbird, to switch from automatic-pilot cruising to tortuous dogfight maneuvers in the flash of a second. They are not as skilled as, for instance, terns or black skimmers at snatching fish in mid-flight from the ocean's surface, but for scavengers they are very adroit, dispatching the offal tossed from shrimp boats the instant it hits the water, plucking tourist-tossed popcorn out of the air. Their trim, angular wings are designed for sudden twists and turns, and their awkward-looking webbed feet act as in-flight rudders. Goofy and ungainly as they appear on the ground, the sight of these birds crisscrossing the sky above the harbor at dawn or floating languidly overhead like stray thoughts in the afternoon, gives rise to something close to admiration.

○

Chameleons aren't exactly the sort of creature that inspires adjectival grandiloquence either. They are thin, usually green, rather generic-looking little lizards about five to seven inches long, with independently revolving eyes, a long tail, and unevenly long-toed feet. Each toe is equipped with a tiny claw and an adhesive toe-pad, which enable the chameleon to climb tree branches and scale walls; and the back legs, which resemble slender frog legs, are good not only for climbing but for running and jumping as well. The eyes, set in their little turret-like processes, are good for looking in two directions at once, which in the males, at least, seems to mean keeping one eye out for insects and the other for females. The hunt for both appears constant and all-consuming, and each is "taken" in a similar fashion – with a lightning-quick pounce – although once caught, a female tends to submit more placidly to being mounted than does a dragonfly, say, to being eaten.

Chameleons of the sort found in South Texas are not true chameleons, it turns out, but something called green anoles. They lack the prehensile tail of the Old World lizard and are smaller, but they do have the ability to change color, hence their common name. Most of the time they are pale green, but become a brilliant, almost luminescent green when excited, and they can also turn various shades of brown. They do not change color in response to their surroundings, as is popularly thought, but as part of a complex system of purely visual signs and signals that communicate specific intentions and needs. Unlike laughing gulls, who communicate mainly through sound, and at high decibel levels at that, chameleons "talk" to one another in absolute silence, with an assortment of curious body movements and displays. They bob their heads up and down with an action most closely resembling push-ups, extend a bright pink throat-fan that flares and retracts like a pulsing beacon, and otherwise signal one another at considerable distances without making a sound. They are not social creatures like gulls and so do not hang around in groups, and their discourse is more formalized and select. They attract and court mates, establish precisely defined territories, defend them against intruders, all with different formulations of their special code. Gulls rant at one another indiscriminately and without pause, but chameleons send telegrams across space. Their messages are brief, carefully timed, and precisely rendered – the required information, nothing more.

"Anole," I notice suddenly, is an anagram for "alone," and alone is what these creatures seem to prefer. The males do spend much of their time hunting for females, but once the mating takes place, the partners go their separate ways, and even the young are left to hatch and survive on their own. They give the impression of being too busy with more important matters to bother much with each other, and communicate literally on the run. They'll pause just long enough in a jerky scamper across a wall or fence railing to flash some push-up signs or extend their throat-fan, but then they're gone, perhaps leaping into a bush after an insect or scooting along in pursuit of some other ambition. You never see them just loafing and gazing absently into space or chewing the fat with their comrades, like gulls. They're much too wrapped up in their separate activities for that, much too intent on getting things done.

I've never seen a laughing gull or chameleon together, but obviously they wouldn't get along. The gull would be yacking away endlessly about shrimp boat schedules or those thieving terns while the chameleon was trying to pace out its territory or stalk a grasshopper, and finally the lizard would signal impatiently, "QUIET. MUST WORK," to which the gull would respond, "Why-can't-you-just-re-*lax-lax-lax-lax-lax*!" Domestic conflict would be incessant, and divorce between gulls and chameleons would make even humans look steadfast. Chameleons would accuse gulls of being lazy and irresponsible, and gulls would complain that chameleons were impossibly dull.

There is an ancient Mesopotamian myth in which a good-will pact between an eagle and a snake is broken when the eagle makes a meal of the snake's young. Eagles and snakes are of course common in mythologies the world over, and when found in the same story are usually antagonists, the eagle exhibiting those qualities associated with the "higher" world, the snake with the "lower." Eagles are traditionally symbols of power, majesty, courage and the like, whereas snakes are identified with treachery, evil, and deceit. Eagles show up on presidential seals and as the names of football teams and fighter planes, while snakes are blamed for The Fall and are the object of everyone's fear and hate. Together they represent the two halves of the eternal conflict between humankind's higher ambitions and baser instincts.

I wonder whether the world would be any different if, by some strange and comical twist of fate, laughing gulls and chameleons, rather than eagles and snakes, were our emblems of the glorious and the debased. Would governments march as readily and stridently off to war with the web-footed, bowler-hatted laughing gull as their national symbol? Would crusades and inquisitions and witch trials have been necessary to vanquish an enemy whose metaphorical representative was a small green lizard with a penchant for push-ups? What if being companionable, open, and honest were seen as the highest aims to which a person could aspire? What if being taciturn and self-absorbed were the lowest condition into which a person could sink? Might we all be a bit better off with slightly less grandiose notions both of our virtues and our faults? Perhaps – who knows? – that would make this often desolate world of ours a more agreeable place to live.

Cattle Country

*T*hough I'm partly from the West (Colorado), I didn't first see the Grand Canyon until a few years ago when my wife and I flew out to Phoenix from our current home in Tennessee for a four-day conference I was to attend on "Literature and the Environment" at the University of Northern Arizona in Flagstaff. I did not (I'll now confess, both to the conference organizers and the university that employs me) attend the entire conference. Four days? How about four hours? We spent the rest of the time driving around in our little rental car trying to see as much of northern Arizona as those four days minus four hours, on back roads with frequent stops, would permit.

The Grand Canyon was, of course, indescribable and so my description of it stops there. Just go see it. We followed our instincts and did it backwards, rising early and driving in through the east entrance, where most people drive out, so that by the time we reached the south entrance and Grand Canyon Blacktop-Parking-Lot-and-Shopping-Mall "Village" the hoards that were arriving were just a blight to steer our way through and leave behind. How many of them noticed the haze, courtesy of the Navajo Generating Station and other coal-fired power plants in the region? How many of them realized that that beautiful turquoise ribbon way way way down at the bottom of that inverted mountain range is *falsely* turquoise, courtesy of the silt-trapping Glen Canyon Dam upstream?

Three days left and we've got a dilemma. Do we return the next day for a hike in an attempt *really* to see the Grand Canyon (on the too-popular Bright Angel Trail, with dozens of others seeking the same experience)? Or do we say, "Next time the North Rim with our backpacks," and return our budget rental car good and dirty?

Having chosen the latter, the next day we headed for the Navajo and Hopi Indian reservations with the goal of getting off on the smallest dirt roads we could find. No problem. During one five-hour, poorly mapped, fifteen-miles-per-hour-max stretch, we met, I think, three cars – Indians, of course, who steadfastly refused to wave, but who can blame them?

Here's what I've been getting to:

This was magnificent country. We'd stop periodically and listen to a silence that I'll liken (never having heard it) to the silence of outer space. At the top of one ridge we looked out across a panorama of desert land that seemed to reduce to insignificance all panoramas it is possible to imagine.

And so forth.

But there were parts (long parts), interspersed with somewhat "better"-looking land, where I was thinking, a little uneasily, "Man, this is *really* desert. This must be about as deserty as it gets." For miles it was nothing but dirt and a single plant, sagebrush – and in places, not even that much sagebrush. Also deep arroyos, as picturesque as the word itself and so we took pictures, saying, "Grand Canyons in the making," but failing to note that through them wound no streams. Not knowing what I was seeing, and not knowing that I didn't know, just thinking of all this open space as wonderful to behold, still, something didn't seem quite right about this scene. Were some deserts really this barren, this empty, this wasteland-like? Where were the hawks, or at least the turkey vultures and ravens? We bumped along, half lost, delighting in our adventure, yet feeling, on my part, the slow beginnings of a not-yet-nagging doubt.

○

Fast-forward six months to the following December. I'm between semesters and reviewing the reading material for a course I teach each spring called Literature and the Environment (my stated reason for attending that conference), trying to decide whether to keep Edward Abbey's entertaining tirade – originally a speech – about the grazing of privately owned cattle on Western public lands, entitled "Free Speech: The Cowboy and His Cow," or toss it.

The problem is that my Tennessee students, some with farming backgrounds, consistently misunderstand what old Ed is saying.

No, he's not against the cattle industry.

No, he's not a vegetarian (Ha!).

No, he's not talking about your parents' farm. He's talking about the *West*, especially the arid and semi-arid West, and he's talking about *public* land, not *private* land.

But they never seem to get it.

For one thing (now that I'm sitting here thinking about it), there *are* a lot of questions, if you're new to the subject, that the piece raises, like —

What is public land? (Okay, like Abbey says, it's Forest Service and Bureau of Land Management land, but) —

When and why was "public land" created? and —

Why is most of our public land in the West? and —

Why isn't more of that Western land controlled by those Western states? and —

What exactly is the Bureau of Land Management? and —

For that matter, what does the Forest Service do? and —

Why does the federal government allow cattle on those lands in the first place? and —

And —

And —

(Now that I'm sitting here thinking about it, maybe I don't understand Abbey's piece all that well either.)

O

What is public land?

The Articles of Confederation, this country's first constitution (1781-89), was what most Americans — not exactly enamored of a strong central government – wanted at the time. It created thirteen sovereign states and a Congress with little more power than to say, "Would you please do such-and-such [give us some funds, give us some troops, let us *enforce* the legislation you've said we can pass]?" The results were a helpless federal government, the realization that a helpless federal government was not a good idea, and the Constitution and federal government (oh, well) that we have now.

But out of this period did come one solid achievement, the Northwest Ordinance of 1787.

The states were either "landed" or "landless." The landless states had fixed western borders – because other states formed those borders. The landed states, citing their original royal charters, could make claims to western lands sometimes all the way to the Pacific (no one quite knowing, until Lewis and Clark, what that meant.)

This situation did not make happy the landless states (or the land speculators therein), who correctly saw that huge claims to land meant huge advantages to those states claiming it. They argued that the western lands belonged to the nation as a whole, not to certain geographically fortunate states, and that Congress should oversee the administration of those western lands and their eventual formation into additional states.

Much disagreement ensued.

Virginia, however, with the biggest claims (most of the lands north of the Ohio River; this was then the Northwest), decided it wanted union more than division, and seeing that it had way more land than it could handle anyway, ceded its western claims in 1784 to the Confederation, and the other landed states eventually followed suit. This paved the way for the Northwest Ordinance three years later, which set up rules ("Give them schools. Don't give them slavery. Treat the Indians fairly." ...Well, not all the rules were followed) for how future states would be carved out of those ever-growing western lands. (Ever-growing, of course, because of the Louisiana and Florida Purchases, the Oregon Treaty with Britain, the admission of Texas as a state, and the land we stole...excuse me...the land we *acquired* in the Treaty of Guadalupe Hidalgo following that other "preemptive"...excuse me...following the Mexican War.)

That explains, I hope, what public land *is* (federal government "owns" it, then gives it away to the states); it doesn't explain why there's so much public land *left*, and why most of what is left is in the West. (Nor does it explain why you're several pages into an essay entitled "Cattle Country" and I've said next to nothing about cattle. Please be patient. This is complicated. By the time you're finished with this piece you'll never want to see the word "cattle" again.)

Why so much public land (*your* land, remember) left? Well, the short answer is that Congress tried to give it away, but no one wanted it.

Initially, in the government's efforts to settle the West (it needed people out there to give legitimacy to some of that less-than-legitimately-acquired territory), it tried to sell the land. The Preemption Act of 1841 said, "Establish residence on 160 acres, and after six months we'll sell it to you for a buck and a quarter an acre." But that didn't work because who had that kind of money? Certainly not the poor settlers the Act was intended to help.

So next Congress tried the famous Homestead Act (1862): "Establish residence on 160 acres, and after five years we'll *give* you the land."

Flop again.

The Homestead Act, despite its fame, was largely a failure. Not only did most of those poor settlers not have enough money even to set up a farming operation; more importantly, the Act was wrong-headed to begin with. In the moist East, 160 acres was more than enough land on which to raise your cows and chickens and plant your crops. In the arid and semi-arid West, not so. The Homestead Act was a boon to the thieves and frauds (prominent among them the Western cattlemen; we'll get back to this), but the "little" man had little chance of making a go of it on tracts of land too dry for traditional farming and too small for grazing more than a couple of cows.

But our boys in Washington kept trying.

The Timber Culture Act of 1873 said, "We'll give you *another* 160 acres if you'll plant trees on land that isn't meant for trees." The Desert Land Act of 1877 said, "All right, 640 acres, cheap. All you have to do is irrigate land with water you can't find." The Timber and Stone Act of 1878 said, "Rocks and trees! Come on! You can sell rocks and trees!" The Timber Barons liked the tree deal, the Cattle Barons liked the desert land deal, but if you weren't a "baron" you were out of luck.

At about this same time the Great Lakes Forest was being completely decimated, and the fires that followed the destruction were so numerous and so intense (one fire in 1871 incinerated the entire town of Peshtigo, Wisconsin, along with 1,152 of its citizens) that people began to feel that perhaps saving some of our remaining forests made sense. This led to "forest reserves" being established in 1891 and '97 and then to the establishment of the Forest Service in 1905. Public land.

But we've still got all this other land in the West (some 260 million acres of it) that no one much wants except the Barons (and they don't really want it, they just want to exploit it: cheaper that way), so what do we do with that? Sure, lots of it's nice to look at, but how are we going to *use* it? Because we're humans, see, and furthermore Americans, and we can't just preserve land for its own sake, for those plants and animals and rivers and canyons and mountains and deserts and grasslands that we have dominion over – we've got to *do* something with it.

Well, them cowboys out there have been running their cattle on those lands for quite some time now – for free – so since the land isn't good for anything else (the Western states didn't even want it; too much hassle and expense to manage) [1], let's make the whole thing legal and create the Grazing Service (1934), and then in 1946 let's combine that with the

General Land Office to create (give it a nice-sounding name, now, so's people won't get the right idea) the Bureau of Land Management.

O

That's most of your public land (*your* public land): the national forests and the BLM lands. There are also the national parks, the national monuments, and the wildlife refuges, so you're seemingly doing pretty well with all that land you own.

Not so fast. Let's turn our attention back to those cowboys.

Before cowboys there were the Spanish conquistadors, who brought both cattle and mayhem to Mexico. Columbus was actually the first to bring cattle to the New World (the island of Hispaniola) in 1494 on his second voyage, but it was Gregorio de Villalobos who, in 1520, first unloaded cattle onto the continent, near present-day Tampico, Mexico. Villalobos's more famous colleague, Hernan Cortez, also did his part. In 1530, having "defeated" the Aztecs in 1521, he settled into the quiet life (with the help of 23,000 indentured Indians) of raising cows.

Those cows begat more cows – very rapidly on this vast new open range – and since the practice was to let them run free, they ran free through Indians' crops, driving them off their land (which the Spanish were then happy to appropriate) and spreading (by the tens of thousands, further devastating land already devastated by Spanish mining) [2] northward. By the late 1500s, just sixty or so years after the first cow set hoof on the mainland, cattle had so glutted and overgrazed the entire region of Mexico from the southern highlands to the northern grasslands that "natural" checks and balances kicked in and the cows began dying from starvation (Simon 19). More land was needed (not, of course, fewer cows) and more land was available. In 1598 one Juan de Onate, his pockets full of silver-mining money from Zacatecas, set off with 400-plus humans and 7,000 cows to colonize the upper Rio Grande. Thereafter, wherever a new Spanish mission (or pueblo or presidio) was established – in Texas, New Mexico, Arizona, California – there, too, went the cows. Cows and Jesus: food for the body, food for the soul.

Mexico secured its independence from Spain in 1821, Texas secured its independence from Mexico in 1836, and in 1846 Texas became a U.S. state.

Those hardy, half-wild Spanish cattle, eventually called Texas longhorns, thought Texas was just dandy – mild climate, lots of grass, let's multiply. This they did, most especially during the Civil War when everybody went off to fight the Yankees, and then even more so after the Union took control of the Mississippi and supply routes east to the Confederate troops were severed. Those Texas boys came home to...lots and lots of cows. More cows than they had a market for: Western historian John Upton Terrell estimates "probably in excess of six million" (193). Even before the War, much of the market had been just for hides and tallow, not for the beef, which was apparently on the chewy side. Now...what do we do with all these cows?

The lucky break was the railroads, which were gradually working their way west and providing shipping points for cattle driven north – during the brief but fabled "Head 'em up, move 'em out" period – to be transported to lucrative markets back East. Also, after we'd systematically rendered nearly extinct an entire species, the bison, in our efforts, preferably, to render extinct those pesky plains Indians – who just couldn't get it through their heads that this was *our* land, not theirs – the range was open all the way to Canada, so cattle were driven north to fill it back up.

The cattlemen and farmers during this time (the cattlemen called the farmers "nesters") didn't get along too well. Let's say you're trying to scrape out a living on the 160 acres you're homesteading somewhere in the vast openness of Kansas, when all of a sudden here come several thousand head of cattle tromping through your land. Doesn't make for a very friendly howdy-do. Plus, *those* cattle carry Texas fever (later traced to a tick; the longhorns were immune) that causes *your* cows (bred from eastern stock that were brought over with the colonists from England and western Europe) to get sick and die. Then there's this new fencing material, barbed wire – patented in 1874 – which, at first, neither you nor the cattlemen are sure you like. *They* expect *you* to fence your crops in (a practice derived from Spanish law) while *you* expect *them* to fence their cattle in (English law). Most of the western states have passed open-range laws that favor your adversaries, so that when one of *their* cattle – eating up the public domain at the bargain price of nothing – cuts itself up on your new barbed wire fence trying to much down *your* squash and beans, you're the one who gets blamed! (But cattlemen did decide they liked barbed wire. Texas cattle baron Charles Goodnight, for example, illegally fenced up so much public land – 3 million acres – that Teddy Roosevelt finally stepped in and had the fences removed.)

Western cattlemen decided early on that the public domain was theirs, not the public's, and developed the art of whining, coupled with banding together in politically powerful livestock associations, coupled in those days with violence, coupled with fraud, that has served them well right up to the present. Actually, the whining came later; violence and fraud worked better in the early days. After the Indians were forced onto reservations because they were starving because their food source had been eliminated, cattlemen grazed their lands with impunity, used their influence in Washington to have the size of the reservations reduced, then cashed in on the situation by selling to the government the beef that the government fed (minimally) to the Indians. Homesteaders and small stockmen were run off their land and murdered; sheriffs, judges, and politicians (all the way up to Washington) were either public-lands "ranchers" themselves or under the thumb of the livestock associations; and the cattle rustlers of course got theirs – except that, curiously, a lot of those "rustlers" were homesteaders and small stockmen. Public lands were not only fenced and the fence patrolled by range "detectives" (hired guns) – many cattlemen had the audacity to put their completely bogus claims to public land in print. For example:

> *The undersigned hereby notifies the public that he claims the range beginning at the mouth of Double Cross Creek and continuing down the Crazy Horse Valley thirty-six miles to Rabbit Ear Butte, and the entire valley east and west between the Sundown Mountains and the Blue Bonnet Hills.*
>
> *(Signed) Fred R. Smith,*
>
> *Rocking Chair Brand* (Terrell 232)

They complained long and loud about the Homestead Act and its successors, then made use of the Acts to serve their own ends. They'd file a claim to 160 acres along a stream (water was, of course, essential), then have the wife and kids and mom and pop and brothers and sisters and aunts and uncles and cousins also file claims. And/or the cowhands under their employ. And/or waitresses and prostitutes and bartenders and drunks. Result? Nice piece of land with plenty of water.

The Timber Culture Act allowed Western cattlemen to double the amount of land they could obtain fraudulently. The Desert Land Act, which according to Terrell, "was specifically designed to aid the vested interests of the Cattle Kingdom" (212), quadrupled the Homestead Act's original offering. Much of the West, of course, is *not* desert (though more of it is now because of cattle), and the cattlemen's lobby knew that. They also knew that most Americans, and even many congressmen, still *didn't* know it ("Great American Desert" – Zebulon Pike). So what's the best way to scare potential homesteaders away from the most generous land offer of all? Put the word "desert" in the Act's title. As for the irrigation requirement, some homesteaders couldn't even locate any water, or if they could most didn't have the financial resources to build an irrigation system that would enable them to farm the land (almost two-thirds of the claims filed under this Act reverted to the public domain) (Terrell 214). But the cattlemen knew where to find water, and a bucket of water dumped on the ground was sufficient "proof," a million miles from Washington, that you were irrigating it.

Texas had been an ideal cow-incubator because of its plentiful grass and mild climate. No winter forage necessary: just turn your cows loose on the open range year-round. But cattlemen soon realized that even as far north as Wyoming and Montana (buffalo, deer, and antelope had been doing it for thousands of years), you could expect your tough longhorns to fend for themselves during the winter, and usually, on those amazing native grasses, they could.

Usually. There were bad winters, of course, during which thousands of cattle starved and froze to death, and after which animal-lover newspaper editors called our Cattle Barons names, but this was a business, and those were business losses, and most of the time those losses could be absorbed.

Then came the back-to-back winters of 1886 and '87, between which was sandwiched the hottest, driest summer anyone could remember: unprecedented blizzards lasting for days, temperatures dropping to fifty below and staying there...then streams drying up and severely overgrazed ranges burnt to a crisp.

Here's the afore-cited Terrell on the winter of '87, which was even worse than the one before:

> It was said that a man could walk from the Black Hills across the Powder River country to the Big Horn Mountains without stepping off dead cattle. If this was an exaggeration, the estimates of ninety percent loss reported by many companies were not. (253)

Another estimate: 10-12 million cows from 1886 to 1887 dying not very pleasant deaths (Terrell 254).

No complete comeback was ever made from this little slap from Mother Nature – whose consequences were magnified, of course, by the grass-greed of the previous decades. The wanton overstocking of these Western ranges had damaged them to the point that some, perhaps, would never recover.

Damaged how? What does "overgrazed" really mean?

We'll get to that. But first two quick points:

✓... Did those public-lands "ranchers" give up? No way. Not when they'd had it so good for so long. And—

✓... How much beef was actually produced during this post-Civil War period, this cattle-drives-and-cowtowns heyday of the Great American Cowboy, this glorious made-for-Hollywood period of our history that we so cherish? What percentage of the whole? What amount of beef did the fabled Cattle Country produce compared to the rest of the country, where raising livestock was routine, not "romantic"?

Think positive, now. How about citing the most glorious of the glory years, 1880?

15% (Terrell 203).

O

The figure now, for cattle that are grazing Western public lands, is a hair over 2%. When Ed Abbey was yelling about it in 1985, it was...a hair over 2%. The percentages have been minuscule ever since the "heyday," which was also the heyday of the first round of range destruction.

Let's be clear about this: only 2-point-something percent of your beef is coming from cattle destroying *big* percentages of your Western public land.

How much western Forest Service and Bureau of Land management land *is* being grazed by privately-owned livestock?

81% (258 million acres)

Of all the livestock producers in the U.S., how many have federal grazing permits?

3%

Of all the livestock producers *even in the low-producing eleven Western states*, how many have federal grazing permits?

22%

Of that 22%, what percentage of these "ranchers" (mostly rich guys – or corporations – who made their fortunes elsewhere and now want to play cowboy) has gobbled up the lion's share, 65%, of the grazing permits issued by the BLM?

10%

What is the average fee to graze one cow and one calf for one month on Western *private* land?

$11.10

As of 2001, what is the fee to graze one cow and one calf for one month on federal *public* land?

$1.43

How much money does the federal government *receive* each year from grazing fees on federal lands?

$6.5 million

How much money does the federal government *spend* each year *just on killing well over 100,000 coyotes, foxes, bobcats, mountain lions, badgers, bears, and other "predators" (like prairie dogs and beavers) to make the West safe for cows?* (What? You didn't know about this? Well, stay tuned.)

Over $10 million

Total net cost, how much money did the federal government (read federal taxpayer, read you) *lose* on the Forest Service and BLM grazing programs in 2000-2001 alone?

$128 million ("Raw Numbers" 2-3)

○

The cowboys couldn't get something for nothing forever – especially since they'd already wrecked, even for themselves, large portions of that something – so, kicking and screaming, they settled for something for almost nothing.

The first almost-nothing was in 1906 when the Forest Service, a year after its formation, said, "Sorry, boys, starting now it's going to cost you a nickel to graze one cow and one calf for one month on these lands."

What!

But they complied (those that complied) and paid their fees (for the number of cattle they chose to report), and the first public lands grazing fee policy limped along pretty well (if limping is "well") until World War I, when butchering as many cows as possible (open up those lands!) to feed our troops soon to be butchered in Europe took precedence over...well, something milder than butchery?

But why cattle at all in the national forests? Weren't the original forest "reserves" set aside to conserve the forests? How are cows a part of the deal?

Good question.

When all this conservation stuff was being decided, mostly during Teddy Roosevelt's administration, there were two principal schools of thought: 1) give away or sell as much public land as can be "used" in some way by those who want it, and 2) set some of it aside for the future benefit of the public ("benefit" still including "use," but use that could be sustained). Actually, in their underlying assumptions, the two sides weren't that far apart – strict preservationists, "radicals" like John Muir, were rare – and the Forest Service was formed, in part, to better regulate commercial "use," not to prevent it. (Grazing was already happening in the reserves, for example, when they were created.) I can't resist inserting at this point that in the Forest Service "regulating" the timber industry's logging of our national forests would come to mean paying them to clearcut the last of our old growth trees in the Northwest, but that's another issue – sort of.

Meanwhile, regulation of *any* kind regarding those "leftover" 260 million acres wouldn't exist for another 28 years (while the destruction continued), when under the Taylor Grazing Act of 1934, the Grazing Service (BLM predecessor) was formed and that same exorbitant nickle-per-cow charge was levied against the freeloaders. I don't want you to fall asleep on me, so I'm not going to drag you through the particulars of Taylor. Let's just say that it was important in all the wrong ways: under the guise of recognizing that something had to be done about these rapidly-being-ruined "leftover" Western lands, it turned over management of those lands to the foxes (first director, Colorado rancher Farrington Carpenter, then on and on...), and by setting up a system of supposedly-but-not-actually temporary and revocable public-lands leases, it created in the freeloaders' minds the notion that grazing *permits* meant *property* and that "privilege" meant "right."

(The freeloaders, as is probably becoming clear, are adept at talking out of both sides of their mouths. They complain about the Homestead Act *et al*, then use those Acts to further their own ends. They feign outrage at having to "lease" federal land when in fact that's exactly what they want – as long as the fees are kept preposterously low – because the "landlord" is then responsible for most of the maintenance costs. They periodically scream about "returning" federal lands to the states – who never owned them to begin with – because that sounds good and gets everyone excited, but what they really want – certainly not a less well-heeled landlord – is more legislation passed in their favor, which is usually what they get.)

In 1975, in a report to the Senate Appropriations Committee, the BLM itself admitted that only 17% of its rangeland was in good or excellent condition [3], 50% was fair, 23% poor, and 5% bad. Moreover, only 19% was improving, 65% was "static," and 16% was getting worse. The General Accounting Office then upbraided this report for painting too rosy a picture (Ferguson 44).

In 1994 the BLM reported that 34% of its riparian areas were in proper functioning condition, 46% were "at risk" (by livestock), and 20% were not functioning properly. I.e. two-thirds of the most fragile areas for which the BLM is responsible were not in such hot shape (Donahue 174).

And –

"Nearly sixty years after the passage of the Taylor Grazing Act, a study undertaken by the Natural Resources Defense Council and the National Wildlife Federation would estimate that no less than 100 million acres of BLM grazing lands were still in 'unsatisfactory' condition" (Watkins 44).

○

"Unsatisfactory," "fair," "poor," "bad," "at risk," "getting worse." Time to explain what these terms mean.

First of all, cows are not buffalo. Buffalo (more correctly, bison) evolved with the ecosystem of which they were an integral part; cows are domesticated beef-machines, their real-animal ancestor the now-extinct auroch of Europe and eastern Asia (auroch country). "Cattle country" does not exist, and never did, anywhere on the planet. Wherever cattle have been "king," everything else has been reduced to serf status.

Cows are not buffalo (or deer or elk or pronghorn antelope or bighorn sheep), and cows are not a "replacement" for the species we nearly succeeded in wiping out. Buffalo were highly mobile, moving from range to range; cattle are slugs, hanging out in one spot and destroying it. Buffalo had the physiological *capacity* to be mobile, both on long hauls and in swift flights from predators; how often have you seen a cow bolt awkwardly more than a few feet? Buffalo are not nearly as water-dependent as cows; cows hang around a stream until they have trampled the surrounding area (and polluted the stream) into oblivion. Buffalo, because the ecosystems of the West are quite different from those of the Great Plains, were probably never even that widespread in the West; cows...well, that's what this essay is about. And finally, buffalo populations ebbed and flowed with the natural conditions of their environment; cows, like their human coddlers, increase in opposition to their environment ("Just" 295-97).

Today's cattle of course *are* coddled, and have to be. Those hardy longhorns were replaced by tastier but more delicately constituted breeds whose forbears were brought over from England and Europe by the colonists. Forget turning them out to fend for themselves in the winter; they wouldn't make it, and those are losses you *can't* absorb. So winter forage (along with the drugs and hormones) is required, which means conversion of wildlife habitat to monoculture crops of alfalfa and hay, which means (in addition to the habitat loss) even more precious Western water than goes directly to cows (10 to 15 gallons per day per cow) (Jacobs 92) going to irrigate the crops that feed them, the end result of which is that irrigation for livestock forage is the number one agricultural use of water in the West (Wuerthner and Matteson 122).

Half of all the water used in California goes to Los Angeles and San Francisco, right? Wrong. It goes to alfalfa, hay, and pasturage for cows (over 80% goes to irrigated agriculture overall). Colorado bleeds one-fourth of its water onto alfalfa fields (a thirstier than normal plant that needs irrigating late in the season when Western streams are least up to the task). In Montana, more than five million acres are planted in irrigated hay. In Nevada, the driest state in the country...surely it's Las Vegas? Well, no (though let's do get rid of that place as soon as possible – agreed?): again, over 80% of Nevada's water goes to agriculture (irrigated, of course), and most of that is for cows so that Nevada (remember our 2-point-something percent figure?) can compete for 37th place in U.S. beef production with that King of all the Cattle Kingdom states, Vermont ("Guzzling" 195, Ferguson 47).

Since this is the arid West, not the moist East, we've also got a slightly larger than normal problem with evaporation, both from the irrigated lands themselves and from those products of the Bureau of Reclamation's myopic "vision," the Western dams that, in many cases, "would not have been built but for the demand for water storage for irrigation" ("Guzzling" 196). Ed Abbey's favorite dam, which takes its name from the incomparable Glen Canyon – now drowned – created "Lake" Powell (leaving poor John Wesley condemned to flip in his grave indefinitely), which exhales into the desert air 882,000 acre-feet [4] of water every year. That's 6.3% of the average annual yield of the entire Colorado River, which begins in northern Colorado and empties (in a manner of speaking, since there's no river left at that point) into the Gulf of California ("In a Nutshell") [5].

Dams, as Wallace Stegner once succinctly put it, "literally kill rivers" (89). They obviously destroy habitat, they chop up river ecosystems, they alter river flow, they prevent regenerative spring run-off, they concentrate pollutants, they trap life-sustaining silt – all of which says, "You're out" to certain species who belong there and, "You're in" to other species (including exotics) who don't.

In addition to all the problems associated with dams and reservoirs, irrigation for crops often in surplus somewhere else means the "mining" of water from underground aquifers at a faster rate than the water is replaced, and when streams are used for irrigation, lower (or zero) water levels, higher water temperatures, and the reverberant effects of these conditions throughout the entire riparian ecosystem (70-80% of all Western species, animal and plant, are dependent upon riparian zones) ("Guzzling" 196).

But let's get back more directly to our cows. Let's put cows and streams together. Now *that's* a marriage made in heaven.

You're looking at some cows clustered around a stream somewhere in the West. Yes, they've pretty well trampled the hell out of the stream and its banks and the surrounding area where they're clustered, but everything else looks fine: the valley is wide and green, that big blue sky is dappled with the requisite cottony clouds, and look at those mountains in the distance! Look at that snow up there! Man, this is one beautiful scene!

What you're looking at but not seeing – as you couldn't fail to see were you looking at a clearcut or stripmined landscape – is one small part of a very intricate network of destruction.

That 70-80% of all Western species which are dependent upon riparian areas for their survival are dependent upon areas that comprise just 0.5-2% of the entire Western landscape: i.e. a very small support system for lots and lots of stuff (Kauffman 175).

So what happens when you put cows in there?

As cows tromp through, drink from, and urinate and defecate in a stream, they break down the banks. What was originally a deep and narrow stream – perhaps not even visible because of the thick vegetation on both sides – becomes gradually wider and more shallow. With wider and more shallow comes higher temperature – assisted by greater exposure to the sun – so it's "See ya later" to, for example, cold-water native trout and "Come on in" to fish like chub and carp (along with bonuses like algae and noxious bacteria).

Cows are heavy and sluggish and their hooves are hard, and this is not good news for the soils. They become compacted and consequently less porous and absorbent, which means more water leaving town and less staying home; lots more soil than normal leaving town; native plants (after they've been eaten and trampled to death) unable to take root to hold the soil in place; increased stream flow; increased erosion; more collapsing of banks; natural flooding and replenishment of the valley floor, hence watertable, made impossible because the stream, once ecological good buddies with the valley, is now down in the bottom of an ugly gully well below the valley floor; consequent lowering of the water table; consequent drying-up of the stream; consequent replacement in the valley of what *should* be there (native grasses and forbs) with drought-resistant and/or non-native vegetation (such as sagebrush in the first instance and cheatgrass in the second); and – just to throw in a little something "extra," so to speak – no songbirds, since the streamside cottonwoods and willows and aspens have all dried up and blown away for lack of water. (But that's just as well because those birds' winter rainforest habitat in Central and South America is already being eliminated anyway, in large part to make more room for...cows.)

✓. . . Item: "Grazing by livestock has damaged 80% of the streams and riparian ecosystems in the arid regions of the western United States..."

✓. . . Item: "As recently as 1990, a U.S. Environmental Protection Agency report found that 'extensive field observations suggest that riparian areas throughout much of the West are in their worst condition in history...'"

✓. . . Item: In 1994, "a joint Bureau of Land management and U.S. Forest Service report concluded that 'riparian areas have continued to decline' since grazing reforms in the [Taylor Grazing Act] 1930s" (Belsky, Matzke, and Uselman 179).

O

One way that plant ecologists classify the objects of their study is either as "decreasers," "increasers," or "invaders." Decreasers, like perennial bunchgrasses – the original mainstays of grasslands in the West – are native plants that when "disturbed" in various ways by our happy cows decline in density or disappear altogether. Increasers are native plants also (sagebrush and mesquite are good examples) that take advantage of the "disturbance" and move into areas where they don't belong. Sagebrush, for instance, originally comprised "perhaps 20% or less of perennial bunchgrass communities [but] has become the dominant plant and formed essentially closed stands on thousands of square miles of Western rangelands" (Ferguson 92). Invaders are the exotics, the non-native species (like the cows themselves) that not only don't belong where the bunchgrasses once thrived – they don't even belong in North America. All too often their seeds came over on the hides or in the stomachs of cattle. All too often they quickly took over. Why? Because not having evolved on this continent, they didn't have to deal with the competitors and parasites that made them part of the natural balance in Europe and Asia where they did evolve.

Two examples of invaders that everyone has heard of:

✓... Kentucky bluegrass – not native to Kentucky. It spread so fast that by the time settlement was underway in that region, bluegrass was already well established. It proved useful, of course (I'm partial to the musical strain, myself), but some other exotic might not have, and it did replace the native canelands and doubtless many species associated with them.

✓... How about that classic Hollywood emblem of the Old Southwest, those tumbling tumbleweeds? Russian thistle, actually, and this exotic, like so many others that took up residence in the West, did *not* prove useful, except to John Ford.

The overwhelming majority of Western exotic plants, of which there are many, are not numbered among the "useful." They're weeds. Cheatgrass first showed up in Pennsylvania in 1861, then wildfired its way throughout the West, and was firmly established by 1900. Originally welcomed by the cowboys (nutritious perennial bunchgrass), it soon proved itself to be viable as cattle forage for only a brief part of the season, wildfired its way across Western grasslands in more ways than just figurative, and once established, proved impossible to eradicate (Ferguson 94). In the Intermountain West, it now covers 100 million acres, and continues to spread (Donahue 120). Halogeten, a prime example of the many ironies associated with the Western cattle industry, just loves those "disturbed" soils that cattle create – then turns around and poisons the cattle that eat it. It now occupies 11 million acres (Donahue 121). Knapweed, medusahead, salt cedar, yellow star thistle, filaree, pink bull thistle, brown curly dock, leafy spurge – not plants you want to invite to your party.

One exotic, crested wheatgrass, is deliberately – nay, obsessively – seeded by the BLM (on public lands, of course) because it *is* useful – to cows.

(The Bureau of Land Management, by the way, has been re-named by those who don't count themselves among its fans The Bureau of Livestock Management.) By 1990, over15 million acres of Western public land had been planted in this non-native species that hails from Turkestan (Jacobs 249). It depletes soil nutrients in a way that native grasses do not; requires re-seeding (in those damaged soils) every 15-25 years; and in the words of Denzel and Nancy Ferguson in their landmark – and courageous – book entitled *Sacred Cows at the Public Trough*, creates "exotic monocultures [that] amount to little more than biological deserts" (163).

Which brings us to one of the BLM's favorite ironic pastimes: range "improvements." You see, Western grasslands (forgive me if I do not use the anthropocentric and self-serving industry term "range"), after millions of years of trying, just could not get their act together. They needed help from our welfare cowboys and their lackeys in the BLM so that their grass wouldn't be "wasted" on pointless wildlife, so that the hungry multitudes of the United States of America could be provided their 2-point-something percentage of beef. Crested wheatgrass is just one example of the BLM's efforts to "improve" (with the taxpayers' money) on Mother Nature's botched job.

Another is fences (not too many, now; let's just string up, oh, around 600,000 miles-worth) (Jacobs 203), which slice up wildlife habitat (and occasionally the wildlife), and create the impression, in both the freeloaders' minds and the public's, that public land is private land. (But they do provide for the implementation of that much ballyhooed range "conservation" practice, "rest-rotation" grazing, which means, Eat up this here patch of land, then leave it for the wildlife while it "rests" and go eat up that there patch of land, then just about the time that first patch starts to be of some benefit to the elk and deer and antelope, go eat it up again.)

And roads (durn it, we got to have *roads* to get to our *cows*, but we ain't gonna overdo that neither – half a million miles sound about right?) (Jacobs 221), which...slice up wildlife habitat, and open up the land to erosion, which silts up the streams, which...[6]

And a whole laundry list of water "development" projects like bulldozing stock tanks and drilling wells and capping and piping springs to fill stock tanks and water troughs.

And "treating" sagebrush with helicoptered herbicide prefatory to seeding the land with crested wheatgrass – sagebrush that wouldn't be there in such abundance but for the previous overgrazing of the native grasses.

And –

And –

But my favorite range "improvement" is "animal damage control." In fact, I like it so much, it gets the next several pages of this essay all to itself.

O

I believe it was Voltaire who said, "If irony did not exist, it would be necessary for the Western cattle industry to invent it." (Or something like that.)

Thus "range." Thus range "improvements." Thus "treating" sagebrush (and everything else in the "treated" region) to poison. Thus water "development." Thus cattle wrecking the land even for themselves. Thus, in Bernard De Voto's apt characterization of the freeloaders' attitude toward the federal government, "Get out and give us more money" (Stegner 61). Thus something called range management "science," which kowtows to the cowboys. Thus "rest-rotation grazing." Thus "sacrifice areas" (cowshit and mud). Thus elk and bison being blamed for giving to cattle the disease brucellosis, which cattle gave to elk and bison. Thus "Bureau of Land Management." Thus "cattle country" in country supremely unsuited for cattle. Thus "cattle country" and 2-point-something percent.

Thus: the "Animal Damage Control" unit of the Department of Agriculture, U. S. of A.

This could get a little tricky, so perhaps we'd better begin with a good, sound, no-nonsense dictionary definition. Tell us, Daniel:

an·i·mal dam·age con·trol: The "control" – by poisoning, trapping, gassing, shooting, etc., – of animals that *don't* damage the land, and belong there, for the erroneous purpose of "protecting" the animals that *do* damage the land, and don't belong there, and aren't even real animals anyway.

Government involvement in the killing of predators – bounties on wolves, for example – goes back to colonial times, but the involvement was made official in 1931 when Congress passed the Animal Damage Control Act, which authorized the killing of (I'm speaking literally here) everything from ground squirrels to grizzly bears to make the West safe for cows. (The precedent for this Act had already been set when, in 1915, Congress appropriated $125,000 to be used by the old Bureau of Biological Survey – Department of Agriculture – for the same purpose.)

In 1939 the program was moved from Agriculture to the Branch of Predator and Rodent Control in the Department of the Interior; in 1965 it was shifted, within Interior, from Predator and Rodent to the Bureau of Sport Fisheries and Wildlife (which was later renamed the U.S. Fish and Wildlife Service, which for a time was responsible both for killing animals and then, under the 1973 Endangered Species Act, trying to bring back from the brink of extinction some of the same animals they had put there with their killing campaigns); and in 1986 it was moved from Interior back to Agriculture, where, well hidden, it currently remains.

Stand back. I'm now going to hit you with some numbers.

In one 34-year period (1937-70) the *known* number of animals killed by federal employees includes 23,806 bears, 7,255 mountain lions, 477,104 bobcats and lynx, 2,823,056 coyotes, 50,283 red wolves, and 1,574 Lobo wolves. [Subsequently] the red wolf, plus grey wolves, grizzly bears, and two forms of mountain lions had to be put on the Endangered Species List. (Ferguson 138)

In 1989 the Animal Damage Control program...killed 86,502 coyotes, 7,158 foxes, 236 black bears, 1,220 bobcats, and 80 [endangered] gray timber wolves. (Rifkin 209)

Animal Damage Control kill statistics for one year (1991) revealed that *more than 150,000 non-target animals of 23 species* had been destroyed. (Donahue 129). (Emphasis not mine.)

Those are the numbers that were *reported*; when poisons are used (and they're used a lot), the numbers can't possibly be accurate because they're based only on those poisoned animals found; and the numbers do not include all the animals killed (impossible to document, of course, but by some estimates even more than the government kills) (Jacobs 263) by ranchers and their hired hands.

While doing the research for this essay, I became frustrated by my inability to find numbers like those above for years more recent than the late eighties and early nineties. Even Debra Donahue's excellent and exhaustively researched 1999 book *The Western Range Revisited: Removing Livestock from Public Lands to Conserve Native Biodiversity*[7], while loaded with more information than I could ever use, didn't have exactly what I was looking for in the way of recent ADC kill numbers ("kill numbers": sounds so...authoritative, don't you think?). A persistent theme with all the writers I read, in whatever decade they were writing, was "From then to now, no change...From then to now, no change" (except, of course, when killing led to killing *off*, which led to "protecting"). But what if from then to *now*, there *had* been a change? What if things had gotten better? The last thing I wanted to do was yell about a problem that was no longer a problem, or even no longer as much of a problem. I wanted to be able to yell with abandon.

Then I found The Official Website.

Want to know how to get there [8]? No, you won't be able to find it on your own unless you know what you're looking for. Besides, this'll give you a little break before I hit you over the head with more numbers.

○

You've heard of, or read a couple of references to, something called Animal Damage Control, and you think it's part of the Department of Agriculture (USDA)...or Department of the Interior, or Bureau of Land Management, or Fish and Wildlife Services...who's part of what? Anyway, your sources contradict each other as to where it *is*, but you've tried all those other agencies' websites and gotten nowhere, so all that's left is the USDA. (Or maybe this Animal Damage Control thing is just a figment of those radical environmentalists' deranged imaginations because – come on – what you read just seemed too bad to be true.)

So you "Google" (yes, though it pains me to admit, I do "Google") "U.S. Department of Agriculture," and zap, you're instantly in their "home."

Quickest way to find what you're looking for, probably, is just to type "Animal Damage Control" in their "search box." Right?

Well, no. What you end up getting is "more than 1,000 relevant results" that aren't relevant. No agency – just a bunch of documents, each of whose titles contains either the word "animal" or "damage" or "control," but none of them with all three words together.

"Back."

The "menu bar" at the top of the "home page" has, as one of its clickable choices, "Agencies, Services & Programs," so that's what you try next – after noting briefly, as one of today's "Top Stories," that Agriculture Secretary Ann M. Veneman and Interior Secretary Gale Norton (they're women, so they've got to be okay) are just pleased as punch about the Senate's recent passage of what's-his-name's "Healthy Forests Restoration Act." Irony, anyone?

"Agencies, Services & Programs." Well, there's lots of stuff on that page, but no Animal Damage Control anywhere. The most logical of the ten major headings would seem to be "Natural Resources & Environment," under which are listed both "Forest Service" and "Natural Resources Conservation Service," but you're not feeling logical today, you're feeling ironic, plus lucky, because yesterday you won a zillion dollars in the lottery with a ticket you didn't even buy, a gust of wind blew it into your face and it smacked you right between the eyes, just *glued* itself to your forehead, practically *begged* you to turn it in, so instead of "Natural Resources and Environment" you select the heading "Marketing & Regulatory Programs," under which are two sub-headings, "Agricultural Marketing Service" and "Animal and Plant Health Inspection Service" (APHIS), and under the latter are twelve sub-sub-headings, none of which is Animal Damage Control, so that's what you click.

Now you're "home" at APHIS, whose job is "Protecting American Agricultural and Natural Resources." Starting to sound pretty good, except for the "natural" part. You click on "Programs," and up they pop: "Office of the Administrator," "Biotechnology Regulatory Services," "Plant Protection and Quarantine," "Veterinary Services," "Animal Care," "International Services," and (dead last; probably just a coincidence) "Wildlife Services."

Suddenly it comes back to you! The message that was written on the reverse side of the lottery ticket! You didn't understand it at the time, and anyway, all you cared about was the money! It said!

"In its effort to advance from ironic euphemism to disgusting ironic euphemism, the Animal Damage Control Division of the U.S. Department of Agriculture, in 1997, changed its name to *Wildlife Services* and didn't tell anyone."

Home at last!

O

The current (as of this writing) home page of Wildlife "Services" features three photographs left to right of a gray wolf – currently classified as "endangered," but possibly facing a reduction in status (by what's-his-name's administration) to "threatened," which would also reduce its protections; two Canada geese – which are doing just fine, thank you, and in some areas maybe even too fine; a mountain lion – which probably *should* be classified as endangered, but they're so elusive that no one really knows how many are left; and below our three token animals a graphic of a box containing the cryptic question "What is Wildlife Services?" So let's click.

What we learn is that "Wildlife are a valuable natural resource that are looked upon with beauty [looked upon with beauty? don't know as I've ever done that; can't they even fake an expression of appreciation without mangling it?] and enjoyed by Americans across the Nation. But [no sense in wasting time getting to the point] as increased urbanization leads to *a reduction in wildlife habitat* and as *wildlife populations continue to expand* [emphasis mine, only because I find it fascinating how that paradoxical process works], conflicts between people and wildlife are all too frequent. Wildlife can destroy crops, kill livestock, damage property and natural resources, and pose serious risks to public health and safety."

Catch the drift? Ready to defend yourself at all costs against those civilization-destroying wildlife? And that's only the first paragraph.

The rest is just propaganda – euphemism, misleading statistics, indirection, and outright lies – but a couple of recurring "themes" are worth mentioning.

There's quite a lot of politely defensive discussion about lethal versus nonlethal methods of predator "control." We're treated repeatedly, for example, to versions of the following: "While lethal management is necessary in certain situations, considerable opportunity exists for developing effective nonlethal means of managing wildlife damage." "Lethal management" means guns, traps and snares, "denning" (that's a nice one), and a whole smorgasbord of poisons. "In certain situations" means "from the outset and practically always." And "considerable opportunity exists for developing effective nonlethal means" means "We prefer just to kill 'em."

We're also assured that "WS directs its activities only at specific wildlife populations responsible for the damage" and that "WS strives to select the method that will kill the predator in the quickest and most humane way possible." Damned lies. Poisons, traps, and snares kill whatever goes for the bait, and poisons can continue to kill if other animals then feed on the original victim. Neck snares strangle the animal to death. Traps leave the animal to die slowly or be shot or clubbed to death when the WS "agent" finds it (that is, if it hasn't by then escaped by chewing off its own leg). Poisons are never instantaneous and have interesting side-effects like severe vomiting and convulsions. No shooter gets a perfect kill every time, especially when he's shooting from a helicopter, which is very popular with our agents. And denning (killing the young in their dens) can involve, among other things, clubbing, strangulation, flamethrowers, barbed wire snares, metal hooks, suffocation, and poison gas (Jacobs 254-261).

But I promised you numbers.

Under "Information and Publications" on the WS home page, you'll find "WS Annual Tables." Now you're getting warm. You'll find the last seven years' worth of lots of different tables, but "Number of Animals Taken and Control Methods Used by the WS Program, FY [the year]" is what you want. (Interestingly, when you pull this table up, the word "control" is gone, and "taken" is now "killed." Maybe they didn't expect you to get this far?)

The numbers are for the entire country, not just the West, although with predators we're clearly talking mostly the West. They've broken it all down with bureaucratic efficiency into the number of species killed (157 in 2002, not counting feral species, exotics, and "other"); the states in which they were killed; and those "methods used" (18 altogether: 8 involving poisons, 5 involving guns, 4 traps and snares, and then the multi-method "denning"). The grand total in 2002 was 1,590,040 animals, which was really only a middling sort of year; they did much better in 2000 (3,267,839) and 1999 (4,882,515).

One thing that struck me as I looked over these lists was the number of "target" species on them – mostly birds – for whom I could not conjure up even the beginnings of an answer to the question "Why?" True, in many cases (though certainly not all) their "kill numbers" were negligible... but why? Why at all? Why American robins, purple finches, horned larks, shrikes, eastern and western meadowlarks, 6,796 mourning doves [9], common nighthawks, northern mockingbirds, killdeers, upland sandpipers, kingfishers, barn swallows, and 3001 tree swallows? (And why crows, jays, magpies, ravens, and grackles, for that matter? Because they don't sweetly sing?)

Why 6 species of hawk, plus osprey, plus great-horned owl, plus 223 American kestrels, whose prey is rodents and insects?

Why 20 different species of native duck? Aren't hunters and our shrinking wetlands killing them fast enough?

Why woodpeckers – northern flicker, yellow-bellied sapsucker, pileated, golden-fronted?

Why great and snowy egrets, horned grebes, American coots, snow geese, white pelicans, and 5 species of heron?

Why 516 river otters? Why 721 turtles?

And *why* (except that they're ugly) 608 turkey vultures and 1,882 black vultures? Vultures don't hurt anything! They clean the place up!

But I digress. (I guess.) Our focus, let us remind ourselves, is on the predators, the cow-killers, the monsters whose ultimate aim is the destruction of Western Civilization itself. (No, not *that* Western Civilization. The other one – located, for example, in Chugwater, Wyoming). To wit –

The dastardly wolf – murderer of Little Red Riding Hood – which, though its range has been reduced from almost the entire area of the continental U.S. to, in the West, a few pathetic pockets in Wyoming, Idaho, and Montana (and two species, the southeastern red wolf and the southwestern Mexican wolf, rendered all but extinct), *is ravaging its way through the vital western livestock industry!* (And that justifies, you see, the gray wolf's being killed in the numbers shown below at the same time it is classified as endangered.)

The wily coyote – Animal King of irony in the West: overgrazing (at least until it completely destroys the land) *increases* his population by increasing the rabbit and rodent populations (Ferguson 143), and trying to kill him off makes him reproduce *faster* by producing larger litters at younger ages (Fahy and Briggs 247). The coyote is currently the single most persecuted predator in the West, in all the most sickening ways you'd prefer not to imagine.

The omnivorous black bear – eater of practically anything – and on rare occasions, even a cow! – though usually only cow-as-carrion cows. But, well, he's a bear, and bears are bad, so let's kill an average of around 400 a year. (Black Bear's cousin Grizzly Bear, whose diet consists of 70-80% *plants*, is even worse, but we've got him down to 1% of his original range, so he's no problem...until, of course, he takes one step out of Jellystone Park, and then *blam!*) (Jacobs, 268, 265)

The sinister mountain lion – slinking around at night eating preferably deer, but yes, now and then, one of those precious cows. The deer part gets the hunters worked up, too, the fools not stopping to consider for half a second that low "game" populations aren't caused by natural predators (you know, that whole balanced ecosystem thing?) but cows and the co-opting of grasslands, cows and the destruction of grasslands, cows and their introduced diseases, and cows and the carving up of "game" habitat. But anyway, that's too complicated, so for a long time in the West, mountain lions were classified as a "varmint" species, then upgraded to "game" status so that would-be White Hunters could go after them as "trophies" – but not on their own, you understand, since those cats are too smart for humans, but with dogs.

The devious (15-30 pound) *bobcat, the wicked* (13-25 pound) *badger and the conniving* (10-15 pound) *fox.* Are you kidding? Them bloodthirsty devils practically inhale our 1,000-pound cows. Enough said.

And finally (okay, so it's not a predator; it's an animal, ain't it?), *the industrious "varmint" beaver.* It's curious how a species that could play a vital role in restoring those cow-blasted areas – by, with their ponds, raising the water level of the stream, returning natural flooding to the valley, stabilizing the valley water table, reversing the erosion process, and inviting back the desicated vegetation (Fouty 187) – is slaughtered by our "agents" in such consistently wanton quantities. But that's irony for you.

All right, here are your numbers. They represent the last five years for the above-named monsters. (Wildlife "Services" gives you seven years, but that struck me as...overkill.) You can decide for yourself if "From then to now, no change." [10]

	1998	*1999*	*2000*	*2001*	*2002*
Badger	580	601	613	660	607
Beaver	30,973	32,795	31,827	29,312	30,266
Black Bear	377	347	446	388	382
Bobcat	2250	2435	2555	2467	2451
Coyote	77,985	85,938	86,955	88,868	86,360
Fox [11]	6472	6182	6071	5182	4976
Gray Wolf	183	173	174	118	194
Mtn. Lion	337	359	390	386	361

○

My favorite part of the Wildlife "Services" website, the part that will leave no doubt in your mind, if you had any, as to where they're really coming from, is the kid's part. The kid's part? Yes, the heading entitled "Educational Tools." Let's click on it.

First item on the short list that pops up is something called the *North Dakota Reader,* which turns out to be a sort of *Weekly Reader* with a purportedly "wildlife" focus that's flavored with just a dash, just a hint, just a trace, just the teeniest tiniest smidgen, of propaganda. The first two sentences in the short lead article, "Living With Wildlife," are a question, *"Who owns the wildlife in our nation?"* (italics theirs) and its immediate answer, "You do," that both put the natural world in its properly subordinate place vis-a-vis the human one, and provide tacit justification for doing with the former whatever we like. Maybe part of what we'd like to do is protect what we "own"? Well, perhaps, but that's never mentioned. Our *real* responsibility as lords over nature is "managing wildlife problems."

These problems, it turns out, are practically everywhere (as are the words "problems," "conflicts," and "damage" themselves, which appear twenty-one times in the first five short paragraphs). In "A Day in the Life of a Wildlife Specialist," our poor overworked animal-killer, who "already has many stops planned for the day," can't even get out the door of his house before the phone rings three *more* times with three *more* complaints about wildlife "problems." According to the piece previous to this one, animals have the choice of either living in "harmony" or in "conflict" with humans, but it seems that more times than not, the darn things opt for conflict! Mr. Specialist "finishes his busy day by returning calls to other people who have called asking for help," then probably goes home and drops exhausted into bed.

"Reading Charts" opens with a scenario of a fatal plane crash caused by a flock of birds; tests the youngsters' skill in reading the numerical tables that follow with questions like "What predator kills the most lambs?" and "How many kinds of animals were reported as problems?"; and closes with a question clearly intended *only* to challenge students' critical thinking skills: "Do you think it is important to work to keep people safe from wildlife problems? Why?"

In "Case Study: Blackbird Problems," we're introduced to young farmers Tom and Mary, who are confronted one day with the sight of "a large black cloud" headed their way out of the east: *redwing blackbirds*! Worried that the birds will destroy their sunflower crop and leave them unable to pay for their farm, they call you-know-who, who saves the day with loudspeakers and a chemical repellant.

Finally, no *Reader* of any kind would be complete without a crossword puzzle, and this one is no exception. "Wildlife Crossword," via key words and negative connotations, summarizes for the kids what they have "learned."

But "back," there's more on our list, principally another document also entitled "Living With Wildlife," this one with the subtitle "Both Sides of the Coin" (find the other side and you get a prize, maybe). Intended, apparently, for a younger audience than the *North Dakota Reader*, each page of this little printable booklet contains a picture and a bit of educational commentary.

We begin with "sheep rancher Green" finding a dead lamb in his pasture. On the following page are pictured a mountain lion, a coyote, and a bear, with the question (asked in a rather exasperated tone), "Why do these animals sometimes attack livestock?" (Whatever the groundless reason, our government boys can help.)

Next is school bus driver "Ms. Hernandez," who "has a problem." Her bus full of eager young scholars has just screeched to a halt on a beaver-flooded road before a beaver-downed tree. Looking much more blond-Anglo than dark-Latino, her mouth an oval of dismay, Ms. Hernandez is clearly in a fix. The question: "What animal do you think caused this damage?" (Turn the page for the answer.)

On another page..."Early one evening, Mrs. Larson was driving home from work. Suddenly, a herd of _____ sprang out of Farmer Owens' cornfield and ran in front of Mrs. Larson's car. Fortunately, she did not hit the _____. What kind of animal do you think ran across the road?" (What kind of animal do you think built the road?)

"Why are there so many deer in the United States?" asks the next page. Why, indeed? Maybe because their natural predators have been eliminated because of wildlife "conflicts"?

Since every eight-year-old likes to play golf, next we get two pages on "conflicts" (i.e. goose droppings) between golfers and Canada geese. Then birds and planes, birds and crops, birds (cormorants) and catfish farms, followed by the mystifying question, "Why do birds eat fish?" (Geez, I don't know, seems like they'd opt for McDonalds like everyone else.)

And so forth. And no prize since we never found the other side.

But the title of the last item on our "Wildlife Services Educational Tools" list, a coloring sheet, is *genuinely* mystifying. Not the coloring sheet itself (a wildlife collage) – just its title. I've been puzzling over it for days now and cannot penetrate its meaning. A new form of irony, perhaps? Who-gives-a-flip irony? Or maybe a Wildlife Services koan? Anyway, it's far beyond *my* ability to comprehend, and I would think most eight-year-olds' also. Maybe you can make sense of it. Here it is.

"Save the Animals"

O

Odds and ends.

✓. . . "Most predators never attack livestock; most livestock deaths...are not caused by predators. The National Agricultural Statistics Service [under the USDA, same as Wildlife Services] found that in 1995, for example, coyotes caused 1.6% of all cattle and calf deaths, and predators overall only caused 2.7%." Respiratory problems, digestive problems, "unknown" causes, birthing, weather, and "other" each took higher percentage tolls. "Only poison (1.1%) and theft (0.4%) were smaller problems for cattle growers than predation was" (Fahy and Briggs 248).

✓. . . "Field investigations by federal biologists show the major causes of lamb mortality to be premature birth, starvation, and disease; ewes die mainly from birth complications, infections, stress, and disease...Only a few sheepmen suffer severe losses to coyotes, a fact suggesting that human negligence may plan an important role" (Ferguson 142).

✓. . . "In the late 1990s, the cost of killing predators in the western states exceeded *reported* livestock losses to predators by a ratio of three to one" (Fahy and Briggs 247). And reported losses routinely exceed actual ones, for not-so-hard-to-guess federal subsidy and tax break reasons (Jacobs 263, 276).

✓. . . Over 70% of the Western U.S. is grazed by livestock (Donahue 115).

✓. . . The biggest cause of desertification throughout the world is the overgrazing of livestock. "Within the U.S. alone about 225 million acres, or 350,000 square miles (an area about the size of the original thirteen states), have experienced severe or very severe desertification; the area threatened with desertification is almost twice as large" (Donahue 54-55) [12].

✓. . . Cattle in the U.S. produce 750 million *tons* of waste each year (Carter 191). "Nationwide, the output of livestock manure is more than 130 times that of human waste – yet most of the livestock waste enters waterways and groundwater untreated" (Wuerthner 196). "A single cow excretes between 30 and 49 pounds of urine and between 29 and 70 pounds of feces per day, containing 5.4 billion fecal coliform bacteria and 31 billion fecal streptococcus bacteria" (Carter 192).

✓. . . "Producing 1 pound of beef protein often requires up to 15 times more water than producing an equivalent amount of plant protein" (Rifkin 219).

✓. . . "Nearly half the water consumed in the U.S. is used to raise livestock, primarily to irrigate land growing livestock feed" (Schwartz and Matteson 285).

✓. . . "When an average steer is fed 16 pounds of grain and soy, 1 pound is converted to edible meat, while 15 pounds are lost as energy, inedible portions of the carcass, or as waste products" (Ferguson 215).

✓. . . "An acre used for livestock production [i.e. feed] will produce 5 times more protein if planted to cereals [and] 10 times more if planted to legumes" (Ferguson 232).

✓. . . Cattle graze *about half the landmass of the planet* – half of that in pasturage, the other half in "range" (Jacobs 364).

✓. . . "In the tropics, cattle production is responsible for the degradation and clearing of forest on a vast scale, particularly in Latin America. Since 1970, over 50 million acres of moist forest in South and Central America have been converted to pasture" (Schwartz and Matteson 284). "The tragic irony is that the land being cleared and enclosed is poorly suited for grazing. The soil base in a tropical ecosystem is extremely thin and contains very few nutrients...After just a few years of grazing – generally three to five – the soil is depleted" and more land is cleared (Rifkin 195).

✓. . . "Asian adults consume between 300 to 400 pounds of grain a year. A middle-class American, by contrast, consumes over 2,000 pounds of grain each year, 80% of it by way of eating cattle (and other livestock) that are grain-fed" (Rifkin 163).

✓. . . "Despite growing alarm over the problem of too many people fighting for too few resources, little if any consideration is given to one of the most important factors contributing to the crisis. In all of the literature surrounding the issue of over-population, scant attention is paid to the fundamental shift in world agriculture in [the twentieth century] from food grains to feed grains, a shift of monumental proportions whose impact has been felt at every level of human existence" (Rifkin 159).

✓. . . "More than 70% of the grain grown in the U.S. and close to 40% of the grain grown worldwide is fed to animals destined for the plates of the world's more affluent peoples" (Schwartz and Matteson 283).

Odds and ends.

○

But let's return to our freeloaders, our moochers, our parasites, our welfare cowboys, our public lands "ranchers," and their pro-freeloader arguments.

What? They have arguments?

Well, yes, in a manner of speaking (certainly not arguing). I'll list four to which, by now, you can easily respond yourself (space provided; and in keeping with our subject, probably just the word "bullshit" will suffice). Then I'll reply to the last four, and we'll be done with these guys.

1. *We're helping to feed a hungry world.*

Response: _____

2. *Granted, we screwed up in the early days, but now everything is peachy because we've gotten "scientific" with our "range management" practices.*

Response: _____

3. *If livestock aren't allowed to graze the public lands, all those nutritious grasses will be wasted!*

Response: _____

4. *If you run us off the* [public] *lands, the entire* [private] *Western livestock industry will collapse!*

Response: _____

5. *Ranchers are the original conservationists. Why would we destroy our own livelihood?*

Response: Because, a) for most of you freeloader ranchers, it isn't your livelihood; you either have to moonlight with a job in town, or you're some rich bastard (or corporation) who wants to play cowboy in his retirement, and because, b) why worry about acting responsibly when you know that the federal government is going to pick up the tab, after you've wrecked the "range," for all those "range improvements"?

6. *But the local Western economies depend on us!*

Response: No, you depend on them. To repeat, "public land livestock operations yield only tiny fractions of the nation's livestock products, public land ranching is marginally profitable, [and public land] ranching families depend heavily on non-ranch sources of income" (Donahue 268-269).

7. *But...but...tradition! The ranching legacy! Western heritage! Cowboys!*

Response: Don't worry. Once we've booted you off the public lands, those things will still be around. You represent only 22% of all the ranchers in the West. Remember?

8. *All right, you asked for it, you radical-environmentalist, un-American, commie and/or terrorist tree-huggers. Didn't think we had an ace in the hole, did you? Well, start breaking out into a cold eco-sweat when you see these two words: "urban sprawl!" It's either cows or concrete, take your pick! Say goodbye to us freeloaders, and you can say hello to more super-ugly Super Wal-Marts!*

Response: I believe this is called a fallacy. In fact, if my undergraduate philosophy minor memory serves me correctly, this is an example of the "false dilemma" fallacy: either this or that, either black or white, either cows or concrete – the favored reasoning strategy of simple minds. Yes, urban sprawl is a big problem (mainly because people won't stop making babies). No, keeping cows on land where they don't belong, and never belonged, is not the solution. Sprawl, ugly and environmentally destructive as it is, mostly occurs around cities, and cities, though their ecological impact obviously extends far beyond their borders, still occupy, physically, only a tiny part of the West. Cows, and the (irrigated) crops grown to feed them, occupy a vastly larger part.

Also, as already noted, most Western ranchers are not public lands freeloaders, and most of the freeloaders don't derive the bulk of their income from the public lands. "You take away my public lands grazing permits, and I'll be forced to sell the land I do own to the subdivision guys." No, you'll sell or not sell depending upon all kinds of factors unrelated to your grazing permits – starting with the demand, or lack of it, for your land (most city-folk don't want to live in the middle of "nowhere," nor does "nowhere" abound with jobs), and ending with the degree of your own interest in holding on to your land. Good zoning laws and conservation easements will protect open space much more effectively than relying on the goodwill of ranchers, private as well as public, not to sell their land when faced with the financial temptation to do so.

O

Which leaves us with but one last matter to resolve.

Why?

Why, when public lands "ranching" is economically preposterous, politically outrageous, and ecologically insane, is it allowed to continue? Why are an absurdly small minority – a mere quark – of the U.S. population allowed to monopolize, for their own selfish purposes, 360 million acres of *public* land? Why aren't the public lands there for the public? Why aren't they there for the lands? Why aren't they being used as *preserves* for our native species, *preserves* for biodiversity, *preserves* for our last wilderness areas, instead of destroyers of them?

Why?

Why in Hell's name is this still happening?

Good question.

Notes

1. In 1930 Herbert Hoover offered to *give* the federal lands, sans mineral rights, to the Western states. They unanimously turned him down.

2. This was not a new story; sixteenth century Spain was badly deforested and desertified.

3. "A site can have as little as 51% of the expected plants and still be classified as in 'good' condition" ("Understanding" 68).

4. An acre-foot is the equivalent of one acre one foot deep in water.

5. Glen Canyon Dam was *not* built to supply water for irrigation. It was one of the Bureau's "cash register" dams (their term), i.e. a dam whose sole purpose was to make money, through the sale of electricity, to pay for other water projects that could not pay for themselves. For probably the best book ever written on the insane history of water "development" in the West, read Marc Reisner's *Cadillac Desert*.

6. Roads also create a phenomenon known as "edge effect," whereby weedy or "edge-adapted" species invade the "habitat islands" created by habitat fragmentation, to the detriment, in a variety of ways, of the original species. One inadequate example with which to illustrate this complex phenomenon: interior-dwelling red-headed woodpeckers being run out of their holes by aggressive, non-native, and edge-adapted European starlings. The fragmented areas may still have the right number of species – or even more species – but they're the wrong species.

7. Want an indication of the clout (and hair-trigger tempers) that ranching interests in the West still possess? Donahue is a law professor at the University of Wyoming who also has an M.S. in Wildlife Biology from Texas A&M, and has worked for three federal land management agencies and the National Wildlife Federation. According to a March 3, 2000 article in *USA Today*, when her book (published by the University of Oklahoma Press; initial press run, less than 1,000 copies) came out, "the president of the state Senate drafted legislation to close the law school [and] livestock interests demanded that the university board of trustees do a better job of screening faculty [and] questioned how Donahue could use state resources to attack a vital state industry." Said Rob Hendry, president of the (historically infamous) Wyoming Stockgrowers Association: "What the university can do is make sure that their professors don't use university money and university time to

put out that kind of material." Apparently our cowboys are not familiar with the concept of academic freedom.

8. How to get there, that is, as of this writing, late 2003. By the time you read this essay, or by tomorrow, who knows?

9. The numbers are from the 2002 list.

10. And for a more current "now" (2006)... Badger: 511. Beaver: 28,203. Black Bear: 318. Bobcat: 2532. Coyote: 87,476. Fox: 5270. Gray Wolf: 278. Mountain Lion: 346. Also, from 2001 to 2006, the one-month grazing fee on public land for a cow and her calf went up a whole thirteen cents ($1.43 to $1.56), and the federal grazing program continues to lose an average of $123 million a year.

11. "Fox" represents five sub-species: arctic, gray, kit, red, and swift. Two, the northern swift and San Joaquin kit, are currently listed as endangered.

12. "Desertification" is an unfortunate term since a true desert is as viable an ecosystem as any other. Overgrazing creates wastelands, not deserts, so perhaps a better, though no more euphonious, term would be "wastelandification."

Sources

Belsky, Joy, Andrea Matzke, and Shauna Uselman. "What the River Once Was: Livestock Destruction of Waters and Wetlands." *Welfare Ranching: the Subsidized Destruction of the American West*. George Wuerthner and Mollie Matteson, eds. Washington: Island Press, 2002. 179-182.

Carter, John. "Stink Water: Declining Water Quality Due to Livestock Production." *Welfare Ranching*. 189-192.

Donahue, Debra L. *The Western Range Revisited: Removing Livestock from Public Lands to Conserve Native Biodiversity*. Norman: University of Oklahoma Press, 1999.

Fahy, Brooks and Cheri Briggs. "A War Against Predators: The Killing of Wildlife Funded by Taxpayers." *Welfare Ranching*. 247-248.

Ferguson, Denzel, and Nancy Ferguson. *Sacred Cows at the Public Trough*. Bend, OR: Maverick Publications, 1983.

Fouty, Suzanne. "Cattle and Streams: Piecing Together a Story of Change."

Welfare Ranching. 185-187.

"In a Nutshell: Why Glen Canyon Dam Should be Decommissioned." Glen Canyon Institute. info@glencanyon.org

Jacobs, Lynn. *Waste of the West: Public Lands Ranching.* Tucson, AZ: Lynn Jacobs, 1991.

Kauffman, J. Boone. "Lifeblood of the West: Riparian Zones, Biodiversity, and Degradation by Livestock." *Welfare Ranching.* 175-176.

"Raw Numbers." *Forest Magazine.* Special Issue 2003: 2-3.

Rifkin, Jeremy. *Beyond Beef: The Rise and Fall of the Cattle Culture.* New York: Plume, 1992.

Schwartz, Richard and Mollie Matteson. "Eating is an Agricultural Act: Modern Livestock Agriculture from a Global Perspective." *Welfare Ranching.* 283-285.

Simon, Joel. *Endangered Mexico: An Environment on the Edge.* Sierra Club Books: San Francisco, 1997.

Stegner, Wallace. *Where the Bluebird Sings to the Lemonade Springs: Living and Writing in the West.* New York: Penguin Books, 1992.

Terrell, John Upton. *Land Grab: The Truth About "The Winning of the West."* New York: Dial, 1972.

Watkins, T.H. "An Evil in the Season: The Cattleman's Welfare System Begins." *Welfare Ranching.* 41-44.

Wildlife "Services." aphis.usda.gov/ws/http://www.aphis.usda.gov/ws/

Wuerthner, George and Mollie Matteson, eds. *Welfare Ranching: The Subsidized Destruction of the West.* Washington: Island Press, 2002.

Wuerthner, George. "Guzzling the West's Water: Squandering a Public Resource at Public Expense." *Welfare Ranching.* 195-197.

—. "Just a Domestic Bison?: Cattle Are No Substitute for Buffalo." *Welfare Ranching.* 295-297.

—. "Understanding Range Management." *Welfare Ranching.* 67-68.

FOUR:
PUT IT BACK

Overdrive

I test drove the future last week – a "hybrid" – and found, to my not-so-surprised surprise, only the present. The saleslady, who was breathless with excitement over the car's innumerable "features," never even mentioned fuel efficiency or emissions or (yawn) "the environment"; what mattered was all the cool stuff I would get with this car, all the cool stuff it could do. A car key? Please: *so* twentieth century. The "remote keyless entry system with push-button start" is the hybrid way. Nor would I have to turn the "AM/FM/MP3 6-disc CD changer with eight speakers, integrated satellite radio capability and hands-free phone capability" on or off or up or down or sideways; just *tell* it (them) what to do, and your wish is granted. Always had a yearning for "heated outside mirrors"? Well, this car has them. And no longer, after shifting into reverse, must we drag our weary eyeballs six inches skyward to the humdrum rearview mirror; the (standard installation) GPS, right there on the dash, televises the view.

My *Oxford English Dictionary* defines the word hybrid, in its non-biological sense, as "anything derived from heterogeneous sources, or composed of different or incongruous elements." "Incongruous" does, in this case, seem to apply. I felt pretty incongruous driving an "eco-friendly" car that, incongruously, combined "eco-friendly" technology with yet more resource-draining, energy-draining technological trash. I felt pretty incongruous considering the possibility (someone somewhere could figure it out) that more energy was expended developing and manufacturing the car than the car saves in fuel consumption. I felt pretty incongruous wanting something simple when clearly what I *should* want, what I apparently was abnormal in *not* wanting, was as much gadgetry as I could get my hands on.

Yes, the gadgetry is there as an enticement to consumers who would otherwise balk at buying an unconventional car. It is also there because, hybrid or Hummer, Americans just flat want it. We want so much, we Americans. We want, after all, the American Dream. We aren't quite sure what the American Dream *is*, but apparently it involves the accumulation of lots of *stuff*. The car I drove, according to its webpage ad, is "where man's wants and nature's needs agree." Horsehockey. Man's wants are endless, and all nature "needs" is to be left alone. That's not a combination that will "Save the Planet." What *man* needs is finally to grow up. To realize that he's not the only show in town. But we've had about two hundred thousand years to do it. How long will this adolescence last?

Old News

*M*y used copy of *Our Plundered Planet* by Fairfield Osborn (purchase price: $1.95) is a University of Wisconsin Library "discard" complete with call number on the spine, bar code on the back, and library card pocket (sans card) on the inside back cover. A small book, about the size of a trade paperback, it is 201 pages in length with an 11-page bibliography. My copy is a 1952 ninth printing. The book was originally published in 1948.

If neither *Our Plundered Planet* nor "Fairfield Osborn" rings any bells, you are undoubtedly not alone. I'm no expert on environmental literature, but in all of what I'd consider my respectable amount of reading in that genre, I've run across a reference to Osborn's book exactly once (which prompted the purchase) and have since tried in vain to remember where I saw that reference. The book has been out of print for over thirty years, and is apparently all but forgotten. That would be a bitter fate indeed for a book that should be recognized as one of the classics of its genre.

It didn't seem destined for obscurity when it was published. Positively reviewed by the *New York Times*, *New Yorker*, *New Republic*, *The Nation*, and the *Saturday Review of Literature*, it went through numerous initial reprints, and was reissued in paperback in 1968 and again (for the last time) in 1973. Heavily researched but clearly aimed at a general audience, its appeal (well, except for its message, which probably belies my next statement) would seem to be general, too.

But...don't go looking for *Our Plundered Planet* at your local Barnes and Noble.

An internet search of "Fairfield Osborn" is likely to get you his father, not the son. Osborn, Sr. is even in the *Encyclopedia Britannica*, and his face made the cover of *Time Magazine* in 1928. He was an influential paleontologist who gave to *Tyrannosaurus Rex* its name, and was president of the American Museum of Natural History from 1908-1935, during which time he assembled a world-class vertebrate fossil collection. He was also, unfortunately, a proponent of eugenics, from which his son gently distances himself with a single sentence: "The antipathies of nations and races, the cults of 'superior' and 'inferior' races, cannot be founded on biology." (26)

The son was the president of the New York Zoological Society (now Wildlife Conservation Society) and the author of one other book, *The Limits of the Earth* (1953), which is worth reading for its historical value but not, to my mind, as powerful an ethical statement as *Our Plundered Planet*. It is the ethic Osborn advances in his first book that I think lifts it out of the realm of mere historical interest and gives to it (sadly) lasting relevance.

The book is a worldwide survey, continent by continent, of the ways humans past and present have laid waste to the earth – often with unhappy consequences for themselves – and a plea for change both in our behavior and in how we think of ourselves in relation to the natural world. Sound familiar? Sound like something you might have read, say, yesterday? Well, Osborn was trying to call attention to these matters over half a century ago (along with Aldo Leopold, whose *A Sand County Almanac* was published a year later), and while that might be cause for celebrating his prescience, it might also give rise to gloomier thoughts.

With the Dust Bowl years still fresh in everyone's minds, the book's reviewers, perhaps understandably, tended to focus on Osborn's discussion of soils and erosion: the latter's causes (bad agricultural practices, logging, over-grazing) and effects (ruined land, and sometimes dead civilizations), and the absolute importance of preserving the former. But the scope of *Our Plundered Planet*, short though it is, is both wider and deeper than "We must prevent another Dust Bowl." Over and over Osborn reminds us (or tells some of us for the first time?) that nature is not our "enemy" with which we must do "battle," that we do not stand apart from and above the natural world but exist within it, and that all living things are bound together in a web of interdependence that we meddle with only at our peril. He worries about a planet whose natural resources are finite while its human population explodes. He understands not only that most people do *not* understand what we are doing to our globe but that, far worse, they do not care. And he does not share the general public's apparently blind and complacent faith in "the marvels of modern technology" (199) to solve all the problems we have created.

Any book half-a-century-plus old, regardless of how prescient, is going to be dated in certain ways, and *Our Plundered Planet* is no exception. But, "current" facts and figures that are no longer current aside, it is remarkable how right Osborn is even when he is "wrong." For example, he expects 1948's world population of over two billion souls to double in seventy years, when in less time than that it has almost tripled. The move by some in Congress in the late forties to transfer Western public lands to state control (and thence into private hands) didn't happen, but Osborn's discussion of the *real* issue, i.e. the exploitation of "the [federal] grazing lands and these last forest reserves for every dollar of profit that can be wrung from them," (183) couldn't be a more accurate description of the problem as it still exists today. And though the federal agency, the TVA, that Osborn cites as "an effort to harmonize human needs with the processes of nature" (193) ended up making a joke of that goal, time and many instances of corporate malfeasance have proved him correct when he concludes that private industry (and too often the government also) can't be trusted to do right by the environment without statutory "encouragement" from the federal courts.

But Osborn is right more often than when he is "wrong" even nominally. E.O. Wilson put a name to biodiversity, but biodiversity – and the consequences of ignoring its implications – is the central theme of Osborn's book. He anticipates Robert Paine's concept of keystone species (the "killing of other creatures...without an understanding of what they are contributing to the life scheme"), and he warns about the dangers of pesticides, and specifically DDT, more than a decade before Rachel Carson's *Silent Spring*. He calls for international cooperation (à la Kyoto?) in reversing the planet's downward slide, and he finds it:

> extraordinary that with a few exceptions there is no such thing as the general teaching of conservation in our schools and colleges today. The study of history would be illuminated if emphasis were placed on the fact that conditions resulting from man's misuse of his natural living resources were definite factors in the movements of people, and in the origins of wars. Likewise courses in economics, engineering, chemistry, biology, sociology and even philosophy would be vitalized if they included considerations of man's relationships to the natural physical world in which he lives (200).

He even (most eerily to read it now) "predicts" the hurricane Katrina disaster – which was not caused by the hurricane but by the U.S. Army Corps of Engineers' decades-long meddling with the Mississippi River:

> How about the valley of the greatest river of them all, the Mississippi, its bed so lifted, its waters so choked, so blocked with the wash of productive lands, that the river at flood crests runs high above the streets of New

Orleans? As in historical times, the power of nature in revolt will one day overwhelm the bonds that even the most ingenious modern engineer can prepare (190).

Why are books like this always news? Why, if this book is ever reissued, will there be those whose eyes are opened for the first time, and others who scoff arrogantly at Osborn's "doom-and-gloom" message? Why must the message be forever repeated?

Our Plundered Planet should be reissued. Will it help? No. But at least it will be another in the long list of writings that, not so far in the future, our descendants, as they struggle to survive on a planet turned "enemy," can read and ask themselves in bewilderment and anger, *Why didn't they listen?*

Bite

*M*y 1991 trade paperback edition of Edward Abbey's 1982 essay collection *Down the River* features, on its cover, a photograph of a beautiful mountain valley somewhere in the West (the place isn't identified, nor the photo credited) with, "flowing" through its center, not a river but a...reservoir. What a perfect metaphor for all the ways in which Abbey's writing was/is misunderstood: some clown at Penguin Books in NYC can't tell the difference between a living river and a river-that-has-been-dammed (insert pun here), and slaps a picture of a flatwater reservoir (complete with bathtub ring) on the cover of Abbey's book about his river trips! Abbey would have loved the irony.

The received opinion on Cactus Ed seems to be fourfold: 1) he's a "Western" writer and also a "nature" writer and therefore not eligible for membership in the "important" writer club (don't expect his appearance anytime soon in, for example, *The Norton Anthology of American Literature*, especially when there's all that political-correctness debt to pay off); 2) even though he considered himself, first and foremost, a writer of fiction, his best work is in his nonfiction (which helps to keep him down there in the minor leagues, where he belongs); 3) his best known novel, *The Monkey Wrench Gang*, is a fun read but not much more than that; and 4) his "masterpiece," if he wrote one, is his wonderfully lyrical, wonderfully funny/angry book about his "season in the wilderness" in the mid-1950s at Arches National Monument (now National Park), *Desert Solitaire*.

These assumptions appear to have been accepted without question by most of the scholars (I will resist the temptation to put that word in quotes) in a book of critical essays I recently read (well, mostly read; in some cases, the going just got too tough) entitled *Coyote in the Maze: Tracking Edward Abbey in a World of Words* (ed. Peter Quigley). Though the book, says Quigley in his introduction (his own two contributions are actually readable), "was inspired by the wholesale dismissal of Edward Abbey in the arena of 'serious' scholarship" (1), most of the eighteen contributors do little to advance the serious-scholarship cause. They persist in calling

Abbey a "nature writer" (a label he despised); they explicitly or implicitly, and without supporting the claim, allege that Abbey's essays are superior to his novels, apparently meaning by "essays" *Desert Solitaire* since his actual essay collections (*Solitaire* is whole cloth, not an assemblage) are barely mentioned, if at all; they agonize over how to categorize (beyond "nature writer") Abbey's willfully uncategorizeable oeuvre; and like all pedant-scholars, they over-interpret, misinterpret, "see" the invisible, miss the obvious, and articulate their theories in near-inarticulate prose.

Here's SueEllen Campbell, in her contribution to the book, "Magpie," wringing her hands over the fact that Abbey doesn't say much about the Utes in *Desert Solitaire.*

> I was even more troubled to realize that there are only two places in this book where Abbey even mentions the Utes...What can we make of such a stunning omission? Could he not have thought about this? Did he think it didn't matter? Is this something else he found it necessary to repress? How many of Abbey's central premises are built upon this silence? How many of our cultures? (42)

Beats the hell out of me, SueEllen, but maybe he didn't talk about the Utes (or any number of other subjects) because it didn't fit his purpose to do so.

Or here she is making a "connection" between Abbey's comment (in *Solitaire*) about having "seen the place called Trinity, in New Mexico, where our wise men exploded the first atomic bomb" and John Donne: "What bizarre implications of intertextuality might emerge if we also remember that the Trinity site was named after a poem by John Donne?" (43).

Bazarre indeed.

How about Tom Lynch, in his essay "Nativity, Domesticity, and Exile in Edward Abbey's 'One True Home,'" who denies "nature writer" Abbey even his love of nature when Lynch (reading Abbey's mind instead of his words) declares, "For Abbey the great evil of Glen Canyon Dam is not so much that it has submerged a canyon as that it has constrained his freedom" (99).

Or Steve Norwick in "Nietzschean Themes in the Works of Edward Abbey," who, after he has quoted the following passage (again, from *Solitaire*)... "We are kindred all of us, killer and victim, predator and prey, me and the sly coyote, the soaring buzzard, the elegant gopher snake, the trembling cottontail, the foul worms that feed on our entrails, all of them, all of us. Long live diversity, long live the earth!" (34)...concludes, "If Abbey is not a Nietzschean, [this passage is] not only disturbing and puzzling but also repugnant and out of place" (202).

Come again?

Then there's Bryan L. Moore ("From the Banks of the Illisus to the Arches of Utah: Edward Abbey as Noble Rhetorician"), who compares Abbey's "rhetoric" to Plato's: "What I wish to show is that Plato's central ideas on rhetoric provide a still-fertile ground for testing the ethicality of Abbey's persistent, passionate critique on human encroachment of wilderness" (264).

And William Chaloupka, in "Edward Abbey's Inadvertent Postmodernism: Theory, Autobiography, and Politics" (oh, how I love these ruminative titles with...colons), who barely mentions Abbey, so eager is he to show us how much he knows about postmodernist theorists.

And James A. Papa, Jr. ("The Politics of Leisure: 'Industrial Tourism' in Edward Abbey's Desert Solitaire"), who spends his entire time explicating an Abbey essay, "Polemic: Industrial Tourism and the National Parks," that doesn't need explication. (It's a polemic, James! Subtle it's not!)

And Barbara Barney Nelson ("Edward Abbey's Cow"), who, in the worst sort of undergraduate (she holds, of course, a Ph.D.) misunderstanding of how you gather "evidence" to support your "thesis," and with zero appreciation for Abbey's humor, cobbles together isolated, out-of-context, tidbit Abbey quotes to "prove" that – guess what? – Abbey was actually okay with the grazing of privately owned cattle on western public lands.

Two of our scholars, Claire Lawrence and Steve Norwick, get all worked up over the rabbit-braining anecdote (that Abbey invented) in *Solitaire's* "Cliffrose and Bayonets" (which, by the way, is not primarily about "naming," as postmodernist-acolyte Lawrence would have us believe, but about "the unity of opposites," as Abbey explicitly tells us on page 25, and as his title clearly reflects). Both find the incident somewhat shocking (as it's meant to be), but neither seems able to get over it. Ignoring or dismissing Abbey's, again, explicitly worded point ("What the rabbit has lost in energy and spirit seems added, by processes too subtle to fathom, to my own soul... No longer do I feel so isolated from the sparse and furtive life around me, a stranger from another world. I have entered into this one.") (34), and, as "serious" critics, unable to take a joke (Lawrence seems offended by Abbey's reference to "the wicked rabbit," and Norwick solemnly proclaims that his students are able to accept this horrible crime only "if one considers that Abbey is challenging us to accept that we are part of the food chain") (201), they frown their way through their respective analyses [1].

Though most of the writers in this book do acknowledge Abbey's biting humor, few seem able to appreciate it, or even "get" it. Instead, they belabor it to death until one is groaning under the weight of their ponderous observations.

One example:

The last paragraph of Abbey's "Author's Introduction" to *Solitaire* is a caveat...

> Do not jump into your automobile next June and rush out to the canyon country hoping to see some of that which I have attempted to evoke in these pages. In the first place you can't see *anything* from a car; you've got to get out of the goddamned contraption and walk, better yet crawl, on hands and knees, over the sandstone and through the thornbush and cactus. When traces of blood begin to mark your trail you'll see something, maybe. Probably not. In the second place most of what I write about in this book is already gone or going under fast. This is not a travel guide but an elegy. A memorial. You're holding a tombstone in your hands. A bloody rock. Don't drop it on your foot – throw it at something big and glassy. What do you have to lose? (xiv)

Funny, yes? Brash and boisterous, combative, spiked with anger, but funny. (And impressive how he gets all the way figuratively from travel guide to rock.)

Here is Lawrence on this paragraph:

> The most subversive part of the introduction, its last few lines, is understandable not only in terms of Abbey's recognition of the distance between word and object, but also as a deconstructive statement. Abbey craves the referent but sees that his attempt to fix it in words is doomed. The world of which he writes is not static; it is already disappearing: [She then quotes the last half of Abbey's paragraph.] Here Abbey is really playing with the idea of a referent; the world disappears, the book becomes object (tombstone, rock). And he is angry with this state of things. *Desert Solitaire* is a very poor substitute for the desert, the world "out there." This is the comparison that is being made. He also creates a paradoxical reading position with his calling attention to the book as book, hateful object to be thrown at a window or wall. The realistic illusion only works if the reader forgets about language, forgets about the fact that he/she is experiencing reality through a medium. This is the whole idea of transparency; to call this into question by foregrounding textuality is to erase the reader's idea of a real unfolding before him/her and to focus him/her back on language. (160)

And I just thought it was funny.

But enough of this tedious book. Let's turn our attention to a subject that, curiously enough (well, unfortunately, no, not curiously enough), none of our scholars ever addresses except to acknowledge Abbey's superb descriptive powers: his *writing*, his *prose*. As it turns out, Edward Abbey was a *writer*, so it might be a useful exercise to *look* at his writing. Sound like a plan?

"What I wish to show" (harrumph) is that Edward Abbey was a prose stylist of the first order, a word-wizard, and that he reached the zenith of his word-wizardry in his underrated (by the critics) but very popular (with readers) novel, *The Monkey Wrench Gang*.

Prose style. Voice. Tone. Hard things to talk about. (Much easier to talk about "The Inadvertent Postmodernism in the Nietzchean Nativity and Platonic Intertextuality of Edward Abbey's Existentialist Biocentrism: A Load of Horeseshit.") How to describe Abbey's style in *The Monkey Wrench Gang*? Bristling with imagery? Yes. Crackling with detail? Yes. Squirming with wordplay? Yes. Deliberately and delightfully overwritten? Yes. But best, probably, just to show the prose in action.

Three quick examples from the opening chapter of the novel, "Prologue: The Aftermath," in which, during the official bridge-opening ceremony, an "unprogrammed" event – the dynamiting and collapse of the Glen Canyon Dam bridge – takes place:

The heat, and kids eating ice cream…

The people wait. Sweltering in the glare, roasting in their cars bright as beetles under the soft roar of the sun. That desert sun of Utah-Arizona, the infernal flaming plasmic meatball in the sky. Five thousand people yawning in their cars, intimidated by the cops and bored to acedia by the chant of the politicians. Their squalling kids fight in the back seats, Frigid Queen ice cream drooling down chins and elbows, pooling Jackson Pollock schmierkunst on the monovalent radicals of the Vinylite seat covers. All endure though none can bear to listen to the high decibel racket pouring from the public-address system. (1)

The public-address system…

The speech goes on, many rounded mouths, one speech, and hardly a word intelligible. There seem to be spooks in the circuitry. The loudspeakers, black as charcoal, flaring from mounts on the gooseneck lampposts thirty feet above the roadway, are bellowing like Martians. A hash of sense, the squeak and gibber of technetronic poltergeists, strangled phrase and fibrillated paragraph, boom forth with the hollow roar, all the same, of AUTHORITY – (2)

And the aftermath of the "unprogrammed" event...

Like a solitary smoke signal, like the silent symbol of calamity, like one huge inaudible and astonishing exclamation point signifying surprise! the dust plume hangs above the fruitless plain, pointing upward to heaven and downward to the scene of the primal split, the loss of connections, the place where not only space but time itself has come unglued. Has lapsed. Elapsed. Relapsed. Prolapsed. And then collapsed. (7)

This is clearly over-written, clearly over-the-top prose. Where one image will do, Abbey gives us three. Where one carefully placed, Hemingwayesque detail should suffice, Abbey gives us half a dozen. Where simple words would be "better," Abbey gives us big ones. In other words, the exact opposite of what every aspiring writer is told constitutes "good writing." But it works! Why? Because Abbey, at his best, is every bit as much in control of his prose as Hemingway was at *his* best. How many of the sentences from the above three passages would you like to cut? What would happen to those passages if you "pared them down" to their essential elements?

The second reason Abbey's high octane prose works is because, quite simply, it's funny. Imagine *The Sun Also Rises* or *A Farewell to Arms* being written in this way: not possible.Though both novels do contain a fair amount of (understated) humor, they are finally very grim indeed. Abbey "overwrites" successfully because, a) he knows exactly what he is doing, and b) a big part of what he is doing is making us laugh.

This point seems lost on our scholars. In fact, Ann Ronald, in the only book-length critical study of Abbey to date, *The New West of Edward Abbey* (1982), actually sees his word wizardry as a "flaw":

If *The Monkey Wrench Gang* has a flaw, it is one of excess. Adjectives piled on top of lively nouns and adverb-laden action verbs describe each activity – "Gobs and gouts of burning slag fall through space, flaring hotter as the descent accelerates, and splash with a steaming sizzle into the water. Fragments of red-hot welded steel and broiled concrete follow" – and the activities are many (190).

She cites the scene in Chapter 12, "The Kraken's Arm," in which the gang is observing, from a safe distance, Peabody Coal's massive, and massively destructive, coal-mining operation on the Navajo Reservation's Black Mesa. And for what? thinks Doc, at which point Ronald quotes the following passage:

Why, to light the lamps of Phoenix suburbs not yet built, to run the air conditioners of San Diego and Los Angeles, to illuminate shopping-center parking lots at two in the morning, to power aluminum plants, magnesium plants, vinyl-chloride factories and copper smelters, to charge the neon tubing that makes the meaning (all the meaning there is) of Las Vegas, Albuquerque, Tucson, Salt Lake City, the amalgamated metropoli of southern California, to keep alive that phosphorescent putrefying glory (all the glory there is left) called Down Town, Night Time, Wonderville, U.S.A. (173)

Ronald's comment: "Unfortunately Abbey inadvertently loses part of his effectiveness when he writes like this, spitting propaganda staccato-style. When his inner rage overrides his control, his prose rhythm accelerates so quickly that the result, like the preceding extract, pounds cacophonously on the reader's ear" (199).

And that passage isn't *meant* to pound "cacophonously" on the reader's ear? Nor do I see Abbey's "inner rage [overriding] his control": any writer knows that a flood of prose like the above is composed at a trickle's pace (Abbey complained at one point in his journal that "MWG proceeds, limps along, much too slowly...A difficult book") (*Confessions* 233), and if "rage" means "humorless," I beg to differ with Ronald on that point, too. Bitter humor, yes; no humor at all, no.

Where did this prose style, this voice, this controlled comic craziness, come from? We seem to see it for the first time, full blown, in *The Monkey Wrench Gang*, Abbey's fifth novel. But I think there are hints of it earlier, in Abbey's "serious" novels, and in *Desert Solitaire* (book number four) we see it finally taking shape.

In Abbey's second novel, *The Brave Cowboy* (I haven't read his first, *Jonathan Troy*; Abbey himself called it a "terrible book" (*A Voice*), and that's good enough for me), we get occasional passages like the following (as Jack Burns walks into the bar that ends in a fight that lands him in jail):

He paused at the door; around him was the brilliance and gold and blue of the light, the sky, the white purifying heat, the withering leaves of the cottonwoods, the dust, and the fragrance of tamarisk along the irrigation ditches. He went in and found a dusky coolness, darkness, the smell of beer, the smell of wine, the smell of Mexicans and dogs and the unemployed. The act of entering the bar was like entering a grotto, leaving the real or perhaps imaginary world outside in the dust and air. (57)

In his third book, *Fire on the Mountain,* a better novel overall (better dialogue, tighter narrative control), not as much of this kind of prose is evident (perhaps because it is a first-person retrospective whose narrator is not given to "raging"), but it does occur, most notably in this passage:

> Well – the summer rolled on, hot and dry and beautiful, so beautiful it broke your heart to see it knowing you couldn't see it forever: that brilliant light vibrating over the desert, the purple mountains drifting on the horizon, the pink tassels of the tamarisk, the wild lonely sky, the black buzzards soaring above the whirlwinds, the thunderheads that piled up almost every afternoon trailing a curtain of rain that seldom reached the earth, the stillness of noonday, the sight of the horses rolling in the dust to wash off the sweat and flies, the glamorous sunrises that flooded plain and range with a fantastic, incredible, holy light, the cereus cactus that bloomed and closed on one night only, the moonlight slanting through the open door of my bunkhouse room, the sight and sound of cool water trickling from a spring after a long day in the heat – I could list a thousand things I saw that I'll never forget, a thousand marvels and miracles that pulled at something in my heart which I could not understand. (97)

But it is in *Desert Solitaire*[2] that we see whence – stylistically and comically – *The Monkey Wrench Gang* came.

It is well known that Abbey purportedly was annoyed by all the attention *Solitaire* received at the expense, he felt, of his novels. He claimed to have just thrown the book together by cannibalizing his journals (he claimed a lot of things, for example that he lived in "Wolf Hole," Arizona, which doesn't exist), but a careful reading of the book reveals that it is written with just as much attention to detail and structure – and with more writerly maturity – as his previous books[3]. Paradoxically, though (and this, I suppose, is just speculation on my part, though I have read all the novels save the first, most of the nonfiction, the edited journals, both biographies, and Abbey's friend Jack Loeffler's memoir *Travels With Ed*), since Abbey, in *Desert Solitaire*, was "just" writing nonfiction, he allowed himself to write fully, and for the first time, in his own voice, which led him to his full *discovery* of that voice, to which he then gave free comic rein in *The Monkey Wrench Gang.*

Three *Solitaire* examples (in addition to the "Author's Introduction," to which I have already referred):

Predators...

We need more predators. The sheepmen complain, it is true, that the coyotes eat some of their lambs. This is true but do they eat enough? I mean, enough lambs to keep the coyotes sleek, healthy and well fed. That is my concern. As for the sacrifice of an occasional lamb, that seems to me a small price to pay for the support of the coyote population. The lambs, accustomed by tradition to their role, do not complain; and the sheepmen, who run their hooved locusts on the public lands and are heavily subsidized, most of them as hog-rich as they are pigheaded, can easily afford these trifling losses. (31)

Rangers…

Put the park rangers to work. Lazy scheming loafers, they've wasted too many years selling tickets at toll booths and sitting behind desks filling out charts and tables in the vain effort to appease the mania for statistics which torments the Washington office. Put them to work. They're supposed to be rangers – make the bums range; kick them out of those overheated air-conditioned offices, yank them out of those overstuffed patrol cars, and drive them out on the trails where they should be, leading the dudes over hill and dale, safely into and back out of the wilderness. It won't hurt them to work off a little office fat; it'll do them good, help take their minds off each other's wives, and give them a chance to get out of reach of the boss – a blessing for all concerned. (55)

And, in a "rage" (an imagined admonition to the tourists) of the sort Ann Ronald would presumably find unacceptable…

Look here, I want to say, for godsake folks get out of them there machines, take off those fucking sunglasses and unpeel both eyeballs, look around; throw away those goddamned idiotic cameras! For chrissake folks what is this life if full of care we have no time to stand and stare? eh? Take off your shoes for a while, unzip your fly, piss hearty, dig your toes in the hot sand, feel that raw and rugged earth, split a couple of big toenails, draw blood! Why not? Jesus Christ, lady, roll that window down! You can't see the desert if you can't smell it. Dusty? Of course it's dusty – this is Utah! But it's good dust, good red Utahn dust, rich in iron, rich in irony. Turn that motor off. Get out of that piece of iron and stretch your varicose veins, take off your brassiere and get some hot sun on your old wrinkled dugs! You sir, squinting at the map with your radiator boiling over and your fuel pump vapor-locked, crawl out of that shiny hunk of GM junk and take a walk – yes, leave the old lady and those squawling brats behind for a while, turn your back on them and take a long quiet walk straight into the canyons, get lost for a while, come back when you damn well feel like it, it'll do you and her and them a world of good. Give the kids a break too, let them out of the car, let them go scrambling over the rocks hunting for rattlesnakes and scorpions and anthills – yes sir, let them out, turn them loose; how dare you imprison little children in your goddamned upholstered horseless hearse? Yes sir, yes madam, I entreat you, get out of those motorized wheelchairs, get off your foam rubber backsides, stand up straight like men! like women! like human beings! and walk – walk – WALK upon our sweet and blessed land! (233)

Abbey wrote three more novels after *The Monkey Wrench Gang*, and several collections of essays. Thumbnail assessments? Well, of the novels, I didn't like his "futuristic Western" *Good News* and can hardly remember it. (Sorry if that's not much of a scholarly critique, but that's all I'm interested in mustering up.) *Hayduke Lives!* – rushed to completion and published posthumously – is, in a word, uneven. The new characters are just as colorfully drawn as Doc, Hayduke, Seldom, and Bonnie were originally, but Abbey seems unable to revive his fab four: they read like cardboard cutouts of themselves. (Perhaps if he'd had more time...?) But Abbey's big novel, his "fat masterpiece," as he called it, the autobiographical *The Fool's Progress*, at which he worked, off and on, for years and years, deserves, I think, to be ranked with *Solitaire* and *Monkey Wrench* as one of his three very best books. Alternating between the hills of West Virginia and the desert Southwest, and between first and third person, and by turns hilarious (with high octane prose to match), grimly funny, and not funny at all, it will, at the very least, take you for a ride. Parts of it, from a gut-wrenching emotional standpoint, are not easy to read, especially toward the end (I was reminded, unsettlingly, of Malcolm Lowry's *Under the Volcano*), but...once you begin the book, you have no choice but to keep going, and the ending is one of the most poignant conclusions to a novel I've ever read.

And the essays? Well, the scholars, as usual, are wrong. Abbey's best work is not in his nonfiction, as we're so often told. Nor (as we're never told) is it in his fiction. Abbey's best work is in (*surprise!*) his best work. And his best work just might bite you in the ass.

In a scene from *Desert Solitaire*, ranger-Abbey, making his morning rounds, comes across a "cautionary note," written by "someone," on the inside of a campground toilet door:

Attention: Watch out for rattlesnakes, coral snakes, whip snakes, vinegaroons, centipedes, millipedes, ticks, mites, black widows, cone-nosed kissing bugs, solpugids, tarantulas, horned toads, Gila monsters, red ants, fire ants, Jerusalem crickets, chinch bugs and Giant Hairy Desert Scorpions before being seated (31).

That "someone" was undoubtedly Ed Abbey, who either really did write that outhouse warning or, much more likely, penned it for his book.

And, yes, I'll be happy to sit down.

Notes

1. What I tell my own students is, "Look, if it'll make you feel any better, Abbey made it up." (Grateful sighs from a few of the females.) "But why did he make it up? How does it contribute to what this essay is about?" And someone always comes up with the answer, which has never included a reference to the "food chain."

2. I'm skipping *Black Sun*, Abbey's fourth novel (novella, really; 157 pages in length), which appeared in 1971, between *Solitaire* and *Monkey Wrench*. It is Abbey's one attempt at a love story, and is embarrassingly sentimental and self-indulgent. In short: ick.

3. Examples from one *Solitaire* piece only, "The Dead Man at Grandview Point": the way that this essay's somber first paragraph (even its first *word*, "Somnolence") sets up the essay's theme of solemnity and death; and the fact that Abbey changed the location of the actual dead man's body from Upheaval Dome to Grandview point, some fifteen miles south, because he wanted the latter as the dead man's perfect "jumping off place" into eternity; and the fact that Abbey has the vulture at the end of the essay looking, not at the dead man earlier but at Abbey himself later, which both personalizes and universalizes the theme of mortality; and the fact that the final fifteen-line paragraph, a gradual pulling-back of the camera as we watch Abbey far below "through those cruel eyes," is comprised of a single ever-widening panoramic sentence.

Sources

Abbey, Edward. *The Brave Cowboy*. New York: Avon, 1956.

—. *Desert Solitaire*. New York: Touchstone, 1968.

—. *Fire on the Mountain*. Albuquerque: University of New Mexico Press, 1962.

—. *The Monkey Wrench Gang*. New York: Perennial, 1975.

A Voice in the Wilderness: Edward Abbey. Dir. Eric Temple. Canyon Productions, 1993.

Peterson, David, ed. *Confessions of a Barbarian*. Boston: Little, Brown and Co., 1994.

Quigley, Peter, ed. *Coyote in the Maze: Tracking Edward Abbey in a World of Words*. Salt Lake City: University of Utah Press, 1998.

Ronald, Ann. *The New West of Edward Abbey*. Albuquerque: University of New Mexico Press, 1982.

This Rock

I have this rock that I picked up somewhere on my random travels last summer, and that now sits in my house without a vocation. It is a fairly nondescript rock even as rocks go, its color a grayish, chalky white – limestone of some sort – and it's fist-sized and has a similar shape. Its one notable feature is the mass of round, bumpy nodules that cover its surface. They look like sea shells at first, but on closer inspection are not; they are the fossilized deposits of tiny, primordial-soup life forms whose name I've now forgotten but whose leavings are the reason I picked the rock up. The rock is, in fact, a chunk of fossilized ooze, and consists entirely of these irregularly-sized nodules that are bunched and clumped together with sea-bottom sediment. It feels odds, now that I think about it, sitting here at my desk in front of my fancy PC with, beside me, a piece of the muck from which I arose.

But the rock is no great shakes of a rock despite its bumps. It has been broken off sharply on three sides, which gives it the look of *part* of a rock instead of a whole one; the brown earth-stain on its underbelly will not wash off; and it doesn't have a side on which it will sit reasonably flat so that I could put it to some practical use, say, as a paperweight. This rock has no real "good side" at all, but looks equally obtuse and lumpy from all angles. Nor is it a particularly unique type of rock, as I had first thought, but is common over large areas of West Texas and New Mexico; I can't even remember now where I picked it up.

In short, my two-pound memento of an enjoyable trip through the Southwest looks about as prepossessing as a chunk of unmixed cement. The minute I got it home I knew I shouldn't have taken it with me: what to do with it? where to set it down? Other rocks I've dragged home have sooner or later found a new direction in life, but this one just sits on my desk and sulks. It's had almost a year now to adapt to its new environment, but stubbornly refuses to join the team.

I can't just throw it away. For one thing, it's a fossil, and throwing away fossils, even fossils of lumpy sea-muck, seems tantamount to throwing away art. I once rescued a large chunk of petrified wood from an office worker's trash can – I was a graduate student janitor at the time – and have used it as a doorstop ever since. I suppose I could just pitch the thing into a ditch or field somewhere, or toss it into the alley behind my house – but then I might be guilty of upsetting the balance of nature by introducing an alien rock form into the region. What if, at some point in the future, a geologist were to stumble across my rock and, filled with excitement, rewrite the geological record based on his find? I wouldn't want to be responsible for setting back science. Besides, the rock would not be amongst its kind.

What is it about rocks that causes people to pick them up and, with no particular purpose in mind, cart them home? I'm not the only one, I know. Not long ago, I helped a friend haul some hay out to his horses, and among the objects we removed from the bed of his pickup prior to the trip were half a dozen near-boulders, which my friend referred to as "Sharon's [his wife's] goddamn rocks." They were even more ordinary-looking than mine, and, my friend assured me, just as pointlessly gathered. Like him, I had trouble seeing the attraction in these *particular* rocks, but no trouble at all relating to Sharon.

I think there is on the part of the rock-gatherer (as opposed to the bona fide rock hound, which I am not; I don't always know what kind of rock I'm holding) the desire to possess something simple in a simple way, free of complication, free of need. People, of course, cannot be possessed, and certainly not without complication, and cars and houses must be tended to and repaired. Implements of various kinds must be put to use, or in time they begin to reproach you for your neglect – the elliptical machine sitting idle, the two hundred dollar juicer used only once – and even ordinary things like clothes and magazines and house plants must be laundered and read and watered regularly. A rock, on the other hand, is at the same time complete unto itself and – theoretically, at least – totally possessable. It neither cries out to be used like the manufactured goods with which we surround ourselves, nor cries out when we do attempt to make use of it, as humans are likely to do. A rock you aren't required to talk to, or learn how to work, or fix when it declines to work – you can just have it. Thus my response to my parents when, as a child, I would bring home yet another rock and they would ask why I wanted it: "I just want it," I would say, and that was that.

Rocks link us to the earth and to a time when our ties to the natural world were much stronger than they are now, to a time when stones were indeed our livelihood, our weapons and tools. In them, we have a tangible connection to a much different world from the one we inhabit now, and to the much different beings we were when we inhabited that world. Pick up a rock and you are holding in your hand not only eons of time but the strength to withstand it, to persist throughout its infinite span. Though inanimate, rocks live in a sense, for they remain while we sputter and die. They are as close to immortality as *we* will ever get.

Maybe it is because I like thinking about these things that I have never taken an interest, not even when I was young, in those polished gemstones that can be purchased in souvenir shops in those parts of the country where someone like me can be found stumbling around with his eyes on a spot two feet in front of his shoes. Polish up a rock and you erase all signs of its having endured the millennia to arrive at this moment when it catches your eye, and you destroy the link to that older world from which it has traveled and dress it up to suit your own. No facelifts for any of *my* rocks, no makeup for glamorous parts they don't fit. I'll take them as they are, polished only in streams – lumps, bumps, cracks, stains and all.

Which brings me back to this rock I've got sitting on my desk and the problem of what, since it doesn't seem to like its home here, I'm going to do with it. Not all rocks, it turns out, *can* be possessed without complication, for this one has complained from the very beginning. Most of my other rocks have found gainful employment as bookends or paperweights or doorstops or, if nothing else, as just-to-look-at rocks, but it just hasn't worked out between me and this latest one. I guess I'll have to capitulate to its wishes, much as I hate to be bossed around by a chunk of limestone, and take it where I know it will be content.

For, you see, I lied when I said I couldn't remember where I found this rock. I know exactly where I found it, could walk to within three or four feet of the very spot. One day soon I'm going to take this rock and drive back to that spot – park the car next to the leaning speed limit sign that appears to be growing out of the center of the lechuguilla plant, scramble up the short ridge on the west to the overhanging ledge that, from the road, looks like a cave but is not (my reason for climbing up there to begin with) – and put it back.

About the Author

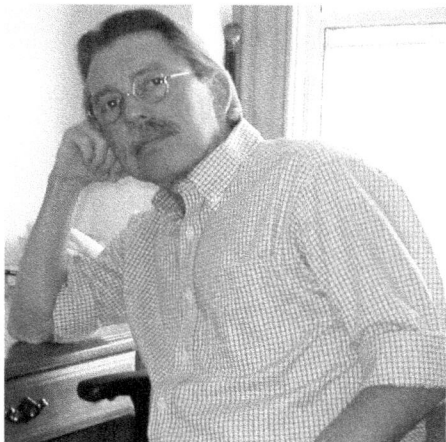

Michael O'Rourke's essays have appeared in *North American Review*, *ISLE*, *Isotope*, *Capitalism Nature Socialism*, *Gettysburg Review*, *New England Review* and other journals, and four of his essays have been cited as "Notable" by the editors of *Best American Essays*. He is a graduate of Colorado State University and the University of Iowa Writers' Workshop and is an English professor at Tennessee Tech University. He lives with his wife Michelle, an ESL instructor, in Cookeville, Tennessee.

About the Artist

Janell O'Rourke, Michael's sister, has exhibited her paintings and drawings in solo and group shows throughout the East Coast. Her most recent exhibitions include: "Nature Spirits," "Degrees of Density," and "Figure? Ground" in New York City. This is her first collection of published illustrations. Janell lives and works in Queens, New York, with her husband, Vicent Evans, a musician, and four superb cats.

www.ingramcontent.com/pod-product-compliance
Lightning Source LLC
Chambersburg PA
CBHW051732020426
42333CB00014B/1271